Furniture Finishes

Like your favorite clothing, your best-loved furniture is a reflection of your personality and taste. It is, moreover, something that can remain beautiful for a lifetime and beyond. Some fine finishes will actually improve with the passing years, acquiring a mature patina that should be lovingly tended with the appropriate wax or polish. Yet even those finishes on which age has taken a harsh toll are rarely beyond redemption; many can be restored to the prime of life by the miracle of refinishing.

In times past, finishing furniture often required enormous skill, exotic materials, specialized workrooms and a degree of patience not given to ordinary mortals. Now, thanks to modern techniques and materials, professional-looking finishes can be achieved at home. You can work wonders with wood stain and shellac, varnish and lacquer; even such seemingly arcane procedures as veneering and inlaying are within your reach. Indeed, if you undertake some of the projects in this book, you may well find that the battered old table you were going to throw out, or the scarred, dingy chair acquired from a secondhand store, has become a prized treasure — the very piece that evokes the most admiring comments from your friends.

And you will discover other kinds of magic: With carefully selected paint colors, you can make underscale furniture seem larger and oversized pieces smaller, or bring coherence to a disparate collection. Paint can also elicit fun and fantasy: Vinegar painting, marbleizing, stenciling and antiquing are just some of the techniques available for turning plain surfaces into works of decorative art.

The effects of such efforts can be seen in the sampling of expertly wrought furniture finishes presented on the following pages — a gallery of photographs from America and Europe that demonstrate how the choice of a finish is dictated both by the piece itself and by the setting in which it is displayed.

A contrapuntal play of paint finishes lends decorative appeal to this Greek bedroom. Flat pale blue unifies the larger pieces of furniture, while a high-gloss black accentuates the lithe lines of the chairs.

In a Swedish country dining room, the disparate elements of furniture, walls, floor and woodwork are brought together by a common color. The flat gray enamel, chosen for its becoming modesty, makes an ideal foil for pretty table settings.

In this Italian dining room a grand expanse of butter-toned maple has been fashioned into a sleek tabletop with finishing techniques ranging from fine sanding to bleaching and wax polishing. The wood base and chairs are all painted with semigloss lacquer applied so thinly that the wood's natural grain shows through. Transparent acrylic varnish covers all with invisible armor.

By means of different finishes, woven fiber-cord chairs are transformed from identical twins into congenial siblings in a New York City loft. The chair on the left is painted with flat pale blue, in the manner of oldtime porch wicker; that on the right retains the original bronze metallic paint applied in the 1920s.

Late-18th Century traditions of veneering and lacquering come together in the fine Dutch sideboard of an Italian living room. The veneering combines blond satinwood with rosewood banding. The lacquerwork — painted floral motifs on wood panels — was produced in Japan and applied to the doors. The antique side table is also veneered. French polish puts the final bloom on both pieces.

The warmth of old wood glows through the low-gloss clear finish of this game table in a French home. The frames of the chairs have been antiqued with white paint. In the background, an imposing armoire is colored with a blue paint that has grown thin with centuries of age. The combination of soft finishes, at once tranquil and elegant, establishes the room's mood.

The rich, ruddy tones of aged chestnut illumine the shellacked surface of an 18th Century table in Massachusetts. A lustrous black paint, showing the gentle wear of age, defines the chairs at the table. Mock graining, applied in feather strokes, dresses up the surfaces of the simple blanket chest in the left foreground.

Other Publications:
THE ENCHANTED WORLD
THE KODAK LIBRARY OF CREATIVE PHOTOGRAPHY
GREAT MEALS IN MINUTES
THE CIVIL WAR
PLANET EARTH
COLLECTOR'S LIBRARY OF THE CIVIL WAR
THE EPIC OF FLIGHT
THE GOOD COOK
THE SEAFARERS
WORLD WAR II
HOME REPAIR AND IMPROVEMENT
THE OLD WEST

*For information on and a full
description of any of the Time-Life Books
series listed above, please write:*
Reader Information
Time-Life Books
541 North Fairbanks Court
Chicago, Illinois 60611

This volume is one of a series that features home decorating projects.

Furniture Finishes

by the Editors of Time-Life Books

TIME-LIFE BOOKS □ ALEXANDRIA, VIRGINIA

Time-Life Books Inc.
is a wholly owned subsidiary of
TIME INCORPORATED

FOUNDER: Henry R. Luce 1898-1967

Editor-in-Chief: Henry Anatole Grunwald
President: J. Richard Munro
Chairman of the Board: Ralph P. Davidson
Corporate Editor: Jason McManus
Group Vice President, Books: Reginald K. Brack Jr.
Vice President, Books: George Artandi

TIME-LIFE BOOKS INC.

EDITOR: George Constable
Executive Editor: George Daniels
Director of Design: Louis Klein
Editorial Board: Roberta Conlan, Ellen Phillips,
Gerry Schremp, Gerald Simons, Rosalind
Stubenberg, Kit van Tulleken, Henry Woodhead
Editorial General Manager: Neal Goff
Director of Research: Phyllis K. Wise
Director of Photography: John Conrad Weiser

PRESIDENT: Reginald K. Brack Jr.
Senior Vice President: William Henry
Vice Presidents: Stephen L. Bair, Robert A. Ellis,
John M. Fahey Jr., Juanita T. James, Christopher
T. Linen, James L. Mercer, Joanne A. Pello,
Paul R. Stewart

YOUR HOME

SERIES DIRECTOR: Gerry Schremp
Deputy Director: Adrian Allen
Designers: Edward Frank (principal),
Albert Sherman, Susan K. White
Series Administrator: Barbara Levitt
Editorial Staff for *Furniture Finishes*
Text Editors: Jim Hicks, John Newton,
Peter Pocock, David Thiemann
Staff Writers: Janet Cave Doughty, Margery A.
duMond, Allan Fallow, Adrienne George, Karin
Kinney, Glenn Martin McNatt, William Worsley
Copy Coordinator: Robert M. S. Somerville
Art Assistant: Jennifer B. Gilman
Picture Coordinator: Renée DeSandies
Editorial Assistant: Carolyn Wall Halbach

Special Contributors: Lynn R. Addison,
Robert Agee, Sarah Booth Conroy, Donald F.
Earnest, Betsy Frankel, Kathleen M. Kiely,
Wendy Murphy, Richard Russell, Susan Wright

Editorial Operations
Design: Ellen Robling (assistant director)
Copy Room: Diane Ullius
Production: Anne B. Landry (director),
Celia Beattie
Quality Control: James J. Cox (director),
Sally Collins
Library: Louise D. Forstall

Correspondents: Elisabeth Kraemer-Singh (Bonn);
Margot Hapgood, Dorothy Bacon (London);
Miriam Hsia (New York); Maria Vincenza Aloisi,
Josephine du Brusle (Paris); Ann Natanson
(Rome). Valuable assistance was also provided
by: Elizabeth Heasman (London); Mary
Johnson (Stockholm).

THE CONSULTANTS

Frederick L. Wall, a furniture maker and sculptor,
is an instructor in furniture design at the Corcoran
School of Art in Washington, D.C. His work has
been featured in many exhibits and publications.
Mr. Wall has been responsible for designing and
building many of the projects in this volume.

David Adamusko has taught woodworking
technology and antique furniture restoration
techniques at the Smithsonian Institution since
1973. He also restores antiques professionally
and is a consultant on furniture restoration
and cabinetwork. Several examples of his work
appear in this book.

First printing. Printed in U.S.A.

Published simultaneously in Canada.
School and library distribution by Silver Burdett
Company, Morristown, New Jersey 07960.

TIME-LIFE is a trademark of
Time Incorporated U.S.A.

Library of Congress Cataloguing in
Publication Data
Main entry under title:
Furniture finishes.

  (Your home)
  Includes index.
  1. Furniture finishing. I. Time-Life Books.
II. Series: Your home (Alexandria, Va.)
TT199.4.F87 1985   684.1'043   84-25280
ISBN 0-8094-5512-9
ISBN 0-8094-5513-7 (lib. bdg.)

CONTENTS

Step-by-step stratagems for perfect finishes

The amber glint of shellacked oak, a flash of peacock blue lacquer, the lustrous reddish face of newly varnished mahogany — all these lovely effects and more are within reach of your paintbrush or sprayer. As this book explains, wood furniture can be given many beautiful finishes, providing you plan carefully for every stage — even thinking through the sequence for applying the finish to the various parts of the furniture (*opposite and pages 18-19*).

The plan begins when you choose a finish that will complement your decorating scheme. With unfinished furniture — whether made at home or in a factory — almost anything is possible. You might stain or bleach the wood (*pages 27-29*), then treat it with a clear shellac, varnish or lacquer (*pages 42-45 and 48-49*). For a more assertive effect, you might just as easily enamel the piece or lacquer it (*pages 46-47*) in any of myriad colors. If dramatic results are your aim, you then can add stencils, vinegar paint, fake marbling or bamboo decorations (*pages 56-87*). And if you have your heart set on elegance, you might give the piece a veneer of rare wood or a topping of gold-tooled leather (*pages 88-113*).

With already-finished furniture, the first question may be whether the piece needs a new finish or not. Antiques — according to the U.S. Bureau of Customs, objects made 100 or more years ago — are best left alone if their defects are minor, or entrusted to professional restorers.

On collectibles of less vintage, as well as on nearly new pieces, you can repair surface flaws yourself (*pages 120-122*) and refinish the piece with enamel or lacquer — or attempt to revive the old finish by cleaning it. Start by giving the furniture lemon-oil rubs. If imperfections persist, try mineral spirits, testing it first on a hidden corner of the piece. This mild, petroleum-based solvent may damage some finishes, but it will restore others by lifting off the film left by years of accumulated dirt, oils, wax and the like. Or switch to a commercial furniture refinisher, which will gradually remove built-up layers of finish. Should all these measures fail to restore the finish to the standards you set, your recourse is to strip off the old finish (*pages 34-35*) and apply a fresh one.

The finishing process starts with preparation of the surface, the foundation upon which the finish is built. Besides sanding (*pages 22-23*), bare wood may need filling and sealing (*pages 24-26*) to make it a slick base for the kind of glass-smooth finish you want. Even then, getting the best results requires understanding your materials and the techniques for handling them. Experiment on scrap wood or an unseen part of the furniture — the inside of a drawer, for example — until you are sure of yourself.

When you are at last ready, the order for applying the finish to the furniture will depend on the type and style of the piece. The drawings here and on the next two pages represent typical pieces of furniture, and each one is numbered to show the sequence in which a professional finisher might approach it. Despite the many possible variations, general principles govern:

● Before beginning, remove all hinges, handles and screws, marking them with tape so you can return them later to their places.

● Dismantle a large piece if you can, so you will be able to work on the separate parts at convenient heights.

● For large pieces that cannot be taken apart, assemble a rolling platform by screwing casters to a piece of plywood.

● To prevent future warping and splitting, apply a sealer or finish to the underside of solid-wood chair seats, table and cabinet tops, and the solid-wood rear of bookshelves.

● When possible, place the furniture surface you are working on in a horizontal position. The light will reflect more evenly, giving you a better view of your work.

● Work from the interior of the furniture toward the exterior to avoid smears.

● Work from the top down, just in case there are drips.

● Work on the least obvious parts of the furniture first, gaining experience and skill as you proceed, and end with the most exposed parts.

A sequence for bookshelves. Lay the unit on its back for convenience, or use a stepladder to reach its top shelves. Finish the interior first, treating each shelf section like a box and finishing first the inside top, then the sides, back and bottom (**1**). After finishing a shelf, finish its front edge (**2**). Repeat with each shelf and its front edge (**3-10**). Finish the sides of the unit (**11**), the front of the frame (**12**, **13**), then the cornice, middle rail and pedestal (**14**, **15**, **16**). If the rear of the bookshelves will be visible, finish it also, waiting until the rest of the unit is dry if it must be moved. Repeat the sequence for each coat of each finishing material.

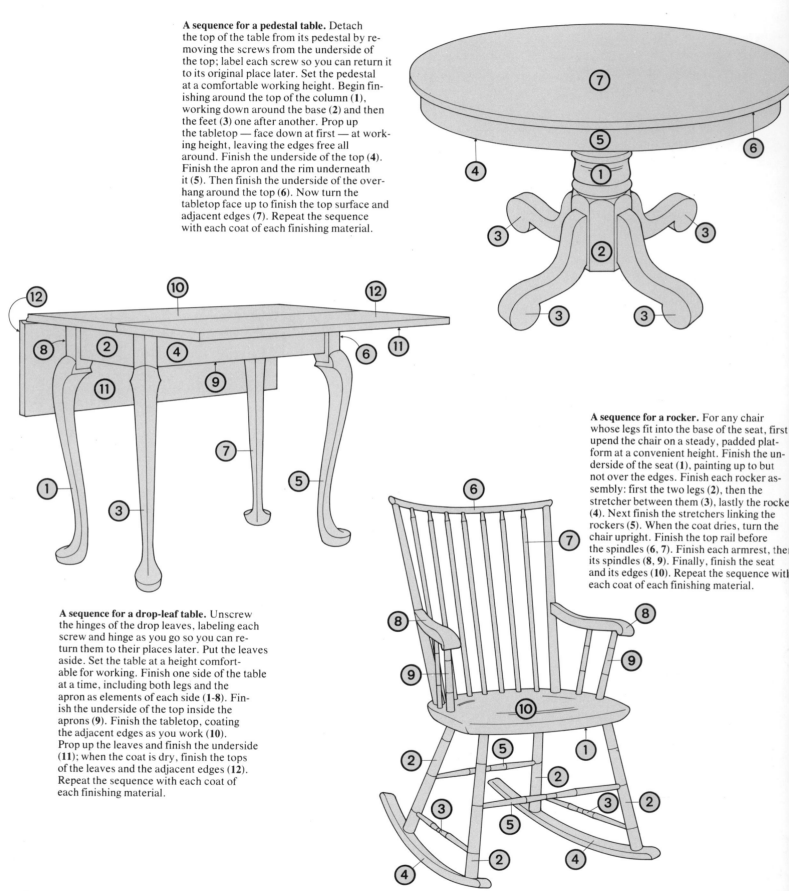

A sequence for a pedestal table. Detach the top of the table from its pedestal by removing the screws from the underside of the top; label each screw so you can return it to its original place later. Set the pedestal at a comfortable working height. Begin finishing around the top of the column (**1**), working down around the base (**2**) and then the feet (**3**) one after another. Prop up the tabletop — face down at first — at working height, leaving the edges free all around. Finish the underside of the top (**4**). Finish the apron and the rim underneath it (**5**). Then finish the underside of the overhang around the top (**6**). Now turn the tabletop face up to finish the top surface and adjacent edges (**7**). Repeat the sequence with each coat of each finishing material.

A sequence for a rocker. For any chair whose legs fit into the base of the seat, first upend the chair on a steady, padded platform at a convenient height. Finish the underside of the seat (**1**), painting up to but not over the edges. Finish each rocker assembly: first the two legs (**2**), then the stretcher between them (**3**), lastly the rocker (**4**). Next finish the stretchers linking the rockers (**5**). When the coat dries, turn the chair upright. Finish the top rail before the spindles (**6**, **7**). Finish each armrest, then its spindles (**8**, **9**). Finally, finish the seat and its edges (**10**). Repeat the sequence with each coat of each finishing material.

A sequence for a drop-leaf table. Unscrew the hinges of the drop leaves, labeling each screw and hinge as you go so you can return them to their places later. Put the leaves aside. Set the table at a height comfortable for working. Finish one side of the table at a time, including both legs and the apron as elements of each side (**1-8**). Finish the underside of the top inside the aprons (**9**). Finish the tabletop, coating the adjacent edges as you work (**10**). Prop up the leaves and finish the underside (**11**); when the coat is dry, finish the tops of the leaves and the adjacent edges (**12**). Repeat the sequence with each coat of each finishing material.

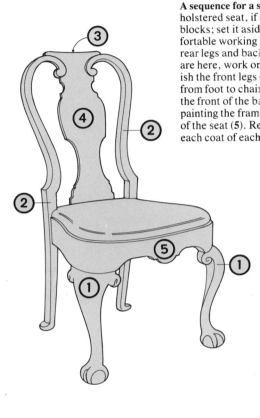

A sequence for a side chair. Detach the upholstered seat, if any, from the frame or glue blocks; set it aside. Set the chair at a comfortable working height. For any chair whose rear legs and back are continuous, as they are here, work on one section at a time. Finish the front legs (**1**), then each rear leg from foot to chair top (**2**). Finish the back and the front of the back splat (**3, 4**) before painting the frame around the sides and front of the seat (**5**). Repeat the sequence with each coat of each finishing material.

A sequence for a cabinet. Remove all hardware — labeling each handle, hinge and screw as you go — and lift off the doors. Take out shelves if they are removable. Set the cabinet at a comfortable working height. Finish the interior — the top, sides, back, bottom and leading edge — as for bookshelves (**1-3**). Finish the ends (**4**) and the back if it will be exposed. Finish the bottom frame (**5**), then the top and its adjacent edges (**6**). Finish the inside surfaces of the doors (**7**) and, when the coat dries, the outside surfaces and edges (**8**). Repeat the sequence with each coat of each finishing material.

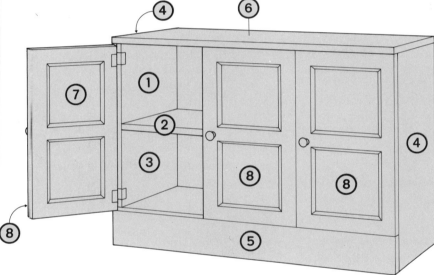

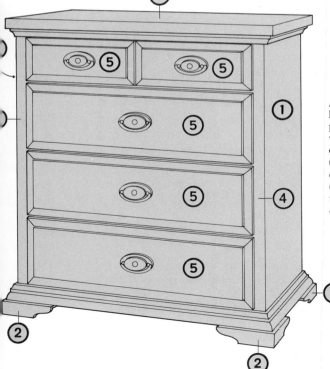

A sequence for a chest of drawers. Remove all hardware, labeling it so you can return pieces to their original places. Set the hardware and drawers aside. Finish the sides of the chest (**1**), then the pedestal and legs (**2**). Finish the top (**3**) with its adjacent edges, and the front frame for the drawers (**4**). Finish the front faces and edges of the drawers (**5**). Repeat the sequence with each coat of each finishing material.

19

Preparations for the finish

The method for preparing a piece of furniture for finishing varies with the features of the piece itself and the finish you want to apply. A deeply pitted tabletop calls for heavy sanding *(pages 22-23)* and a layer of undercoat before it gets enameled. A wood with deep pores will need filling and light sanding to yield a smooth surface *(pages 24-25)*. Most softwoods must be sealed to keep the resin in their knots from bleeding into any kind of stain or finish *(page 26)*. A paint-encrusted chair must be stripped *(pages 34-35)* before you can finish it with varnish.

All these techniques are simple enough if you take the time to read about them first, so you can work out a plan of action that suits your schedule and your furniture. Check the how-to demonstrations in this book, and be mindful of the manufacturer's directions supplied with a product.

Once you know what procedures will constitute your job, assemble tools and materials and set up your work space. Make sure you have enough brushes of the proper types and widths *(box, opposite)*, an ample stock of cheesecloth for pads, and rags of clean, lint-free cotton for wiping up spills. Check that you have compatible thinners and cleaners on hand for your finishing materials.

The nature of the job will help determine the kind of work space you need. An outdoor area is best for working with chemical strippers, which emit toxic vapors, or for heavy sanding, which generates a lot of dust. However, when working outdoors, protect the furniture from rain and dew: Moisture raises wood's grain and necessitates further sanding. Long exposure to strong sunlight can be damaging: Most woods bleach to a lighter shade, and some change color; cherry, for example, reddens with exposure to the sun.

Most final finishes should be applied indoors, where you can more easily control such factors as dust, humidity and temperature. When you set up an indoor work space, make sure you can keep a steady flow of fresh air coming into the room, and can exhaust fumes to the outdoors — not to another room, where they might create a health hazard. Choose a dry, warm area that is small enough for you to keep dust-free, but large enough so you can move around without brushing or bumping the furniture.

Bring in additional lights, if necessary. Experts suggest you have two 40-watt fluorescent fixtures or two 150-watt incandescent lights above your work area so you can see defects such as rough spots or streaks of stain. If you are finishing one piece to match another, check them in light equivalent to that of their eventual setting.

Your jobs will be easier and safer if you keep the work area clean and orderly. Protect the floor with a canvas or plastic dropcloth; newspapers may seem an inexpensive option, but they will in fact behave like blotters and let liquid finishes soak through. Whenever you finish a sanding job, remove dusty floor coverings, and vacuum carefully; otherwise, loose dust will inevitably come to rest on a still-wet finish coat.

Put tools and materials away when you no longer need them, to prevent knocking over open cans of liquids. Keep liquids in tightly sealed metal or glass containers, both to preserve them and to prevent the build-up of vapors that create fire and health hazards. Label containers clearly to avoid confusion when you need to use the materials again.

Remember that many finishing materials are highly flammable (as is always noted clearly on their containers). Keep solvent-soaked rags in a tightly closed metal container to prevent spontaneous combustion. Have a fire extinguisher close at hand. A dry chemical extinguisher is an economical choice; it should be rated for use against Type B fires (flammable liquids, oil and grease). Be certain that everyone working on the job knows how to use the extinguisher, and check it periodically to ensure that it is fully charged.

Proper protective measures can virtually eliminate health hazards from finishing work. When you sand, use a cloth or paper mask to block the dust. If you spray on a finish, wear a chemical-filter mask that removes toxic vapors from the air. Wear rubber or plastic gloves to protect your hands against strippers and solvents. And whenever you use a solvent to wash paint off your hands, use a good lotion to help prevent reddening or cracking of the skin.

An Investment in Brushes

Several brush types, along with foam-tipped applicators, are employed in furniture finishing (right). A foam-tipped applicator is a disposable tool, tossed away after one use. But a brush calls for careful maintenance, which will pay off both in ease of applying the finish and in the quality of the results.

In the past, the best brushes for most furniture finishing were made with stiff hairs from Asian hogs. These resilient bristles have natural splits near the tip that enable them to pick up more paint than smooth hairs would. A "China bristle" brush is still preferred for alkyd and oil-based finishes. But because natural bristles swell in contact with water, bristles made of nylon or polyester are recommended for water-based or latex finishes. Check the ends of the synthetic bristles to be sure they have been flagged — frayed to mimic the split ends of natural bristles.

For delicate and decorative work, artist-brushmakers favor sable bristles. Their suppleness is unrivaled.

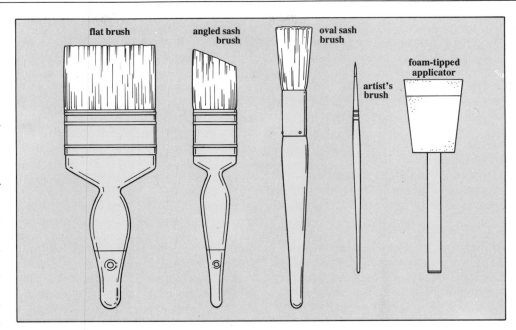

Picking the right brush. A flat brush ½ to 4 inches wide is best for flat surfaces; for detailed work, choose a brush slightly narrower than the surface you are working on. A 1- to 3-inch angled sash brush lets you work in corners without smearing adjacent surfaces. Use a round or oval sash brush ¼ to 1½ inches wide for narrow surfaces and special jobs such as antique glazing (pages 70-73). Artist's brushes of assorted sizes handle intricate details. A 1- to 4-inch foam-tipped applicator is a disposable tool for applying wiping stains or for finishing in tight spots.

1 Cleaning a brush. After each job, wash the brush thoroughly in the solvent recommended by the finish manufacturer by first pouring at least an inch of solvent into a shallow container. Put on rubber gloves, then dip the brush's bristles into the solvent and swirl them back and forth. Remove excess solvent by squeezing the bristles between your thumb and fingers. Keep swirling and squeezing until the bristles look clean, changing the solvent whenever it becomes heavily clouded. Wash the brush with warm water and mild soap until the lather is clean and white, then rinse the brush well. Blot the brush dry with a clean, absorbent rag.

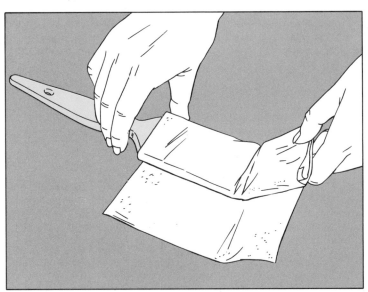

2 Wrapping the brush for storage. Lay the bristles and body of the brush across one end of a long strip of brown wrapping paper. The paper should extend several inches beyond the bristle tips. Fold the paper over the brush, then roll the brush and paper until the brush is encased in three or four layers of paper. Fold the end of the paper up over the bristles, being careful not to bend the bristle tips; crease the paper so it holds its position. Finish wrapping the paper around the brush and secure it with tape or a rubber band. Store the brush on a flat surface or hang it from the hole in its handle.

Sanding for a smooth surface

Thorough sanding is the foundation of a smooth finish, but how much sanding you must do depends on the piece you have. The raw wood of homemade furniture calls for the most sanding. Commercial unfinished furniture is factory-sanded and generally requires only a touch-up to remove dirt, scratches and loose wood fibers. Old furniture about to get a new finish is sanded to expose bare wood and wipe away any surface stains. A valuable antique is never sanded: Abrasion would erase the prized patina only time can bestow.

Though most furniture sanding should be done by hand, a power sander (opposite, bottom right) can be used on large, flat expanses such as tabletops. The best choice is an in-line sander, which works in a straight back-and-forth motion. An orbital sander, which vibrates in a 1/8-inch elliptical path, is acceptable but may leave cross-grained scratches that need to be removed by hand sanding. Avoid disk sanders, which leave ugly swirls, and belt sanders, which tend to gouge.

To sand flat surfaces evenly by hand, exert equal pressure over all areas so as not to create depressions. A sanding block addresses this need by holding the paper flat. Although rubber sanding blocks are available at hardware stores, an equally effective block is easily made from wood scrap (opposite, bottom left).

For rounded surfaces, irregular curves, carvings and turnings, use the edge of folded sandpaper. Around spindles, work long strips of sandpaper back and forth shoeshine-style, as shown at far right.

All sanding should be done in stages, using progressively finer grades of sandpaper. The chart below shows how sandpapers are graded, and which grades perform which steps in the sanding process.

To prepare wood for staining or finishing, you usually need only fine grit and very-fine grit paper, unless the wood is rough. In that case, a preliminary sanding with medium grit is called for. Extra-fine and super-fine grits are generally reserved for the later phases of furniture finishing; polishing with sandpaper between coats heightens luster.

Sandpapers differ in kind as well as degree of fineness. The longest-lasting ones are coated with silicon carbide, recognizable by its grayish black or white color. Aluminum oxide (grayish brown) and garnet (reddish) are also suitable. Flint, which the first 19th Century sandpapers were made of, wears down quickly.

A special technique applies to new unfinished furniture: Before sanding the surface, raise the grain by dampening the wood with water, and sand off the swollen fibers when the wood has dried. Otherwise, surface fibers, flattened during sanding, will rise later to spoil the finish.

Sanding by Hand

sanding block

Sanding a flat surface. Insert a strip of sandpaper into the slotted ends of a store-bought sanding block, or staple the paper to a homemade one (opposite, bottom). Sand in a straight line, with short strokes in the direction of the grain, applying moderate pressure. Work evenly over the surface until the wood is uniformly smooth, before changing to the next-finer paper grade.

Choosing the Right Sandpaper

Description	Grit Number	Use
Coarse	60 80	Leveling uneven surfaces. (Use coarse sandpaper cautiously; it may produce more scratches than it removes.)
Medium	100 120	Removing paint. Preparatory sanding: used in first sanding stage unless surface is unusually rough. Blending shallow depressions.
Fine	150 180	Fine sanding of bare wood. Light sanding of old paint to promote better adhesion of new coat.
Very-Fine	220 240	Light sanding of primer or sealer coats. Final sanding of surfaces to be finished.
Extra-Fine	280 320	Sanding between coats of enamel, varnish or other finishes to eliminate trapped particles and bubbles.
Super-Fine	400	Sanding prior to applying final lacquer coats. Sanding final coats of enamel or varnish to achieve a low-luster finish.

Sandpaper grades. The fineness and use of different grades of sandpaper are shown in the chart at left. Some papers are marketed with only a word description — ranging from coarse to super-fine — printed on the back. Most are numbered: The finer the paper, the higher its grit number. Papers to which the grit is bonded with waterproof adhesive are called wet-and-dry sandpapers; they can be presoaked in water to make them more flexible (page 74).

Removing sanding dust. After each use of sandpaper, sweep the wood surface with a soft whisk broom to brush off any stray abrasive particles that might scratch the wood with further sanding. If you are about to apply a finish coating, wipe the surface with a so-called tack rag *(page 47)*, or clean with a rag dipped in turpentine.

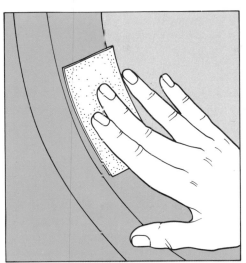

Sanding rounded surfaces. Cut a sheet of sandpaper into quarters; then fold one piece into quarters to form a finger-sized pad. Lightly sand along the grain of the curve, taking care — especially when using coarse grades of paper — not to gouge the wood. When the pad gets clotted with sanding dust, refold it to use another section. After sanding, whisk the surface.

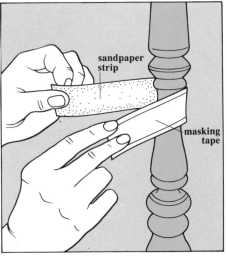

Sanding a turning. Press a strip of 1-inch masking tape to the back of a 1½-inch-wide strip of sandpaper. Pull the reinforced sandpaper back and forth around a turning, working the strip like a shoeshine cloth. Sand evenly along the turning, but do not bother about sanding with the grain: The curves of the turning will hide scratches from the light. After sanding, whisk the surface.

Making a Sanding Block

For a sanding block, you need a palm-sized scrap of 2-by-4; sand off its sharp corners with coarse paper. Cut a rectangle of felt — the kind used for roofing underlay and available at hardware stores — making it slightly smaller than the broad side of the block. Glue the felt to the block to cushion the sandpaper and protect wood from gouges. For each use, cut a piece of sandpaper as long as the block and 5 inches wider, and wrap it around the wood. Staple the paper tight.

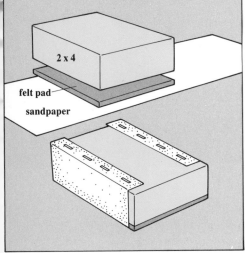

Sanding with a Power Tool

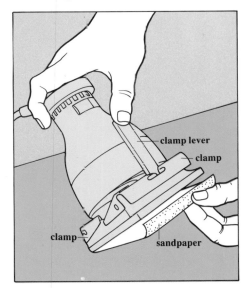

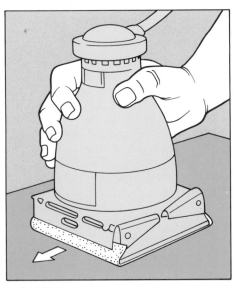

Handling a power sander. To fit paper into the sander — in this case an orbital finishing sander — use the sander's lever to release the clamp, one side at a time, then slip the paper under the clamp *(above, left)* and release the lever. Gripping the sander securely, hold it just above the edge of a flat surface. Turn it on and guide it along the grain *(above, right);* do not press it down. Work in straight back-and-forth strokes, lifting the sander at the end of each stroke. After sanding, whisk the surface. Then hand-sand lightly to take out any scratches.

Filling wood for sheen and color

The glass-smooth surface found on much wood furniture cannot be achieved solely by applying a lustrous finish. Smoothness is generally a built-on effect, and compositions called wood fillers can provide the foundation for such finishes by packing open pores in the wood's surface.

When wood is sawed, the blade slices through hollow cells that carried moisture in the living tree, leaving countless pores. Close-grained woods like pine and fir have such minute pores that only a surface sealer such as shellac is needed to fill them. But others — oak, ash, walnut, mahogany and birch, for example — have larger pores. In many woods, porous areas are interspersed with denser material, where the cell walls grew thick — which is why those woods have pronounced grains.

A finish on unfilled wood soaks into open pores and forms a smooth film only on dense areas. The resulting irregularly textured surface is admired by some for its natural look, but is unsatisfactory to those who want uniform smoothness.

A filler will solve the problem, and it will offer more rewards than mere smoothness. Colored filler can heighten the contrast between the open-pored wood and dense areas. If the piece is being stained, apply the stain first, so it does not loosen or dissolve the filler. Then, unless the filler matches the stain, apply a thin wash of shellac *(Step 1)* to prevent the stain and filler from smudging. People in search of a natural appearance prefer a filler as dark as or darker than the stain, but some like the contrasty look provided by a lighter-tinted filler.

Filler is sold at most paint stores in neutral shades and a few colors; more colors are available from woodworking suppliers. If necessary, you can add stain to a neutral filler to create the color you want *(Step 3)*, but you must use stain compatible with the filler; do not mix alcohol-based spirit stain with oil-based filler. Fillers come in paste form, which must be diluted with turpentine or mineral spirits *(Step 2)*, or as an already-thinned liquid.

There are other compositions called wood fillers, but they serve a different purpose: to fill nail or screw holes and the rough edges of particleboard and plywood. These fillers — wood putty or spackling compound — are applied with a putty knife and then sanded down.

1 **Applying a shellac wash coat.** If you are using a filler of a different color from the stain, prepare and apply a shellac wash coat after the stain and before the filler. Dilute the shellac with 8 parts of denatured alcohol to 1 part of shellac as purchased. Brush it on along the grain in a thin coat, let it dry for half an hour and then sand the surface lightly with very fine (220-grit) sandpaper. Caution: Make sure the sandpaper does not cut all the way through the shellac coat.

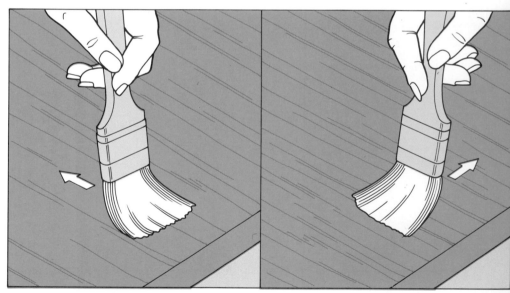

4 **Applying the filler.** Using a brush with stiff bristles about 2 inches long, apply liberal amounts of the filler and press it into the pores of the wood. First brush in the direction of the grain *(above, left)*, then across it *(above, right)*, so that a thick coating of filler covers the surface.

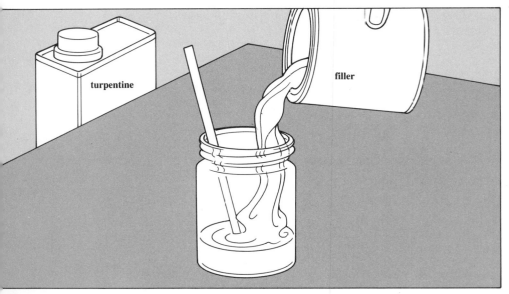

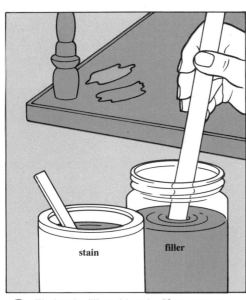

2 **Thinning paste filler.** Stir the filler with a wood stick to blend its ingredients. Pour it into a jar. Add the solvent recommended by the manufacturer — usually turpentine or mineral spirits — a little at a time, stirring constantly, until the filler has the consistency of thick cream.

3 **Tinting the filler with stain.** If you cannot buy filler the same color as the stain you have applied and do not wish to use a darker or lighter filler, you can tint the filler with the stain. Mix stain into the filler in small amounts, experimenting with the color by testing the mix on a hidden part of the furniture — choosing an area that is made of the featured wood — and add more filler or stain to adjust the color as necessary.

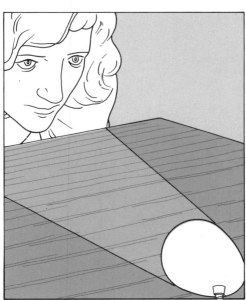

Filling Particleboard

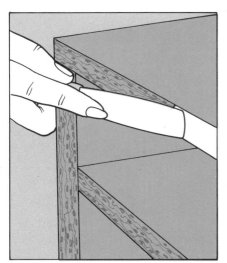

5 **Padding the filler.** Allow the filler to set until it congeals and loses its gloss, but not so long that it dries completely. Using a pad of folded burlap, rub the filler across the grain, applying moderate pressure. This will press the filler into pores and remove the excess. Then lightly wipe along the grain to clean the surface of the wood. Let the filler dry for 24 hours before deciding whether another application is necessary.

6 **Inspecting the pores.** Check to see whether the pores are filled by shining a light across the grain. If you do not see a slight sheen, or if you can discern varying highlights and flat areas, brush on a second application of filler and pad the surface again (*Steps 4 and 5*). Allow to dry for at least 24 hours before sanding with super-fine (400-grit) sandpaper and proceeding with the finish; in cold or humid conditions, the filler may take longer to dry.

Smoothing rough edges. With a putty knife, spread vinyl spackling compound or wood putty onto the edges of particleboard. Pack the filler into the holes and coat the surface with a layer about 1/16 inch thick. Allow the compound or putty to dry overnight. Then sand the edges smooth with fine (150-grit) sandpaper. If the dried filler has shrunk beneath the surface, apply more spackle or wood putty.

Sealing problems out of the finish

Before, during, even after every step of furniture finishing, sealers play important roles. When a natural finish is desired, there are clear and virtually colorless sealers; for enamels and paints, the sealer may be clear or an opaque white or gray.

The primary function of clear sealers is to shield softwood such as fir or pine so it does not absorb too much stain and become too dark. The sealer forms an invisible barrier that stain penetrates slowly and evenly. Clear sealers also prevent softwood resins from bleeding, or running out, into a stain or finish and thus discoloring it. Even when the finish will be opaque, a clear sealer is an essential base coat on softwood.

Applied over stain, clear sealer guards it from solvents in varnishes. Otherwise such solvents might dissolve stain and cause it to bleed and cloud the surface.

A clear sealer is also useful as a solid base for a clear finish on a wood not being filled (pages 24-25) or stained; an opaque sealer serves the same purpose for opaque finishes. To improve the bond of the eventual finish, the sealer is roughened — given what painters call tooth — with super-fine (400-grit) sandpaper.

In addition, some professionals use clear sealers to finish sanding. Even painstaking sanding leaves a microscopic fuzz of wood fibers; further sanding only brushes them back and forth. But sealers saturate, raise and stiffen the fibers so the

sandpaper can cut off the fuzz cleanly

Which sealer you use for any of these purposes depends on the stain or finish you are working with (chart, below) Shellac is a good all-purpose clear sealer it adheres to almost any surface. And most finishes, except those with a poly urethane base, adhere to it. Orange shel lac is preferable on dark woods or stains white shellac best suits light woods.

However, most clear finishes can be di luted to serve as their own easily spread quick-drying sealers. Enamel under coat — typically an alkyd-based coating with a high concentration of pigments and fillers to give it opacity and tooth — suits both enamels and paints. Unlike other sealers, it must dry for up to 24 hours.

Choosing the Right Sealer

Purpose	Stain or finish being used	Recommended sealer	Application method	Dilution
To reduce stain penetration	Alcohol stain Non-grain-raising stain	Shellac	Brush	8 parts denatured alcohol to 1 part shellac
	Penetrating oil stain Nonpenetrating oil stain	Boiled linseed oil	Rag	1 part mineral spirits to 1 part boiled linseed oil
To keep softwood resins from bleeding into stains or finishes; to prevent stain from bleeding into finishes; to give body or adhesion to a finish; to prepare a surface for fine sanding	Shellac, clear lacquer or varnishes other than polyurethane	Shellac	Brush	8 parts denatured alcohol to 1 part shellac
	Acrylic, alkyd or epoxy varnishes	Acrylic, alkyd or epoxy varnishes	Brush	1 part mineral spirits to 1 part acrylic or alkyd varnish
	Polyurethane varnish	Polyurethane varnish	Brush	1 part mineral spirits to 1 part polyurethane varnish
To provide a smooth, uniform surface for paints or enamels; to prepare surface for sanding	Any enamels other than lacquers	Enamel undercoat	Brush	None
	Latex paint	Enamel undercoat	Brush	None

Sealers and their uses. The chart above shows which sealer to use for each of the different purposes that sealers serve, and how to apply them to furniture. Diluted with the proper solvents in the ratios shown, shellac or boiled linseed oil can be used to seal wood before it is stained. Shellac also is a suitable sealer to use as an undercoating for most finishes.

Bleaching the color of wood

Wood, like cotton, is composed of natural fibers that can be bleached. Chemicals that are brushed onto wood can lighten the color of an entire piece or selectively remove spots, objectionable grain patterns and water rings. With enough applications of bleach, dark wood turns bone white.

The weakest bleach is ordinary laundry bleach, or sodium hypochlorite; choose it for removing accidental marks and for lightening woods slightly. Concentrated sodium hypochlorite, sold at paint stores, works best for removing the aniline stains used on most mass-produced furniture; dilute and apply the concentrate according to the manufacturer's instructions.

Oxalic acid, ideal for whitening oak, comes as white crystals that can be dissolved in hot water — 3 tablespoons of crystals to 8 ounces of water. The strongest bleach is the two-part product sold in separate bottles containing special liquid formulations — one of peroxide and the other of caustic soda. The solutions are brushed on the wood one after the other, as shown here, to quickly lighten it.

To be effective, bleaches must soak the wood fibers. The impervious coating of finished furniture, therefore, must be stripped away first *(pages 34-35)*.

Bleach acts differently on various types of wood; be sure to test the effect of your bleach on a hidden corner of the furniture before attempting to treat the entire piece. Always let the wood dry thoroughly — a matter of 12 to 24 hours — before applying another coat of any kind of bleach.

When the wood reaches the desired color, just let it dry if you have used sodium hypochlorite. However, after bleaching with oxalic acid or two-part bleach, you must neutralize the bleach with vinegar to prevent it from reacting with chemicals in finishes you will apply later. With any bleach, sand the dried wood to smooth the grain raised by the liquid.

Bleaching chemicals are caustic; they call for old clothes and demand safety precautions. Rubber gloves and good ventilation are essential. When sanding a bleached surface, wear a dust mask to protect yourself from inhaling the bleach-saturated particles of sanding dust.

1 **Applying two-part bleach.** Pour the two solutions into separate containers. Using a synthetic-bristle brush, spread the first solution — which one to use is indicated on the labels — evenly over the surface. Follow the directions carefully. While the first solution is still wet, use the same brush to apply the second solution over it. Allow the solutions to dry, and then repeat this procedure as often as necessary to lighten the wood to the desired shade. If the bleach does not penetrate evenly by itself, rub each solution in turn into the grain with a plastic-mesh scrubber.

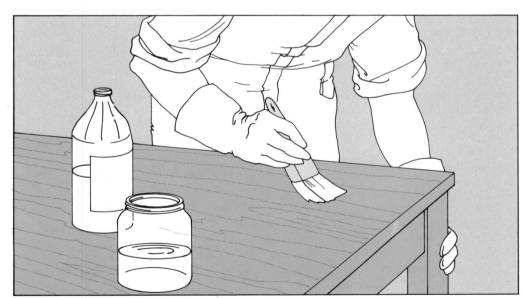

2 **Neutralizing the bleach.** When the wood has reached the desired color and has dried, mix 1 part of distilled white vinegar with 1 part of water to make a neutralizing solution that will stop the action of the bleaching chemicals absorbed by the wood fibers. Brush the solution over the wood and allow it to dry. Then put on a dust mask to protect yourself from sanding dust, and sand the raised grain lightly with very-fine (240-grit) or extra-fine (280-grit) sandpaper — working in the direction of the grain.

A portfolio of woods and stains

Stains change the color of wood while allowing the pattern of its grain to remain clearly visible. They can make an inferior wood look expensive or bring out the beauty in a quality wood by enlivening the natural hues. And they can make one kind of wood resemble another so that at first glance softwoods can pass for more elegant hardwoods.

Although some rich-looking hardwoods, such as rosewood, are too beautiful to tamper with, most hardwoods benefit from staining. The magnificent browns of oak and walnut, for example, can be intensified. And mahogany, which is dull brown in its raw state, fulfills its promise with the help of a reddening stain.

To accomplish all this, stains are available in many formulations *(page 30)* and in a wide range of wood tones from light yellows to dark reds and browns. Both type and color, of course, influence the effect of a stain. But — as the samples at right demonstrate — the wood itself finally determines how a stain looks. Here, all the samples have been treated with a single manufacturer's oil-based stains. Reading from left to right, each row shows how five different woods respond to one stain color; from top to bottom the rows show what four stain colors do to one single kind of wood.

In general, stain works a more intense change in light woods than in dark ones. Porous woods such as oak react more dramatically than relatively impermeable ones such as teak. Softwoods like pine absorb stain unevenly, to end up with light and dark streaks. On the other hand, hardwoods like oak, mahogany, cherry and walnut absorb stain uniformly and hence retain a more natural appearance.

Nonetheless, determining what stain to select for the results you want may require some testing of one or more stains by the methods demonstrated on page 31. If none of the commercial products are totally satisfactory, you can always concoct your own colors by mixing several shades of the same brand or chemical type of stain.

Red Mahogany Stain on Oak

Red Mahogany Stain on Honduras Mahogany

Golden Oak Stain on Oak

Golden Oak Stain on Honduras Mahogany

Cherry Stain on Oak

Cherry Stain on Honduras Mahogany

Dark Walnut Stain on Oak

Dark Walnut Stain on Honduras Mahogany

Red Mahogany Stain on Cherry

Red Mahogany Stain on Pine

Red Mahogany Stain on Walnut

Golden Oak Stain on Cherry

Golden Oak Stain on Pine

Golden Oak Stain on Walnut

Cherry Stain on Cherry

Cherry Stain on Pine

Cherry Stain on Walnut

Dark Walnut Stain on Cherry

Dark Walnut Stain on Pine

Dark Walnut Stain on Walnut

Staining richness into wood

The stains that darken and enliven the color of wood vary not only in color but also in formulation (*chart, below*). Oil-based stains, the most widely available, come in two classes, penetrating and nonpenetrating. Penetrating oil stains carry transparent dyes in solution; these dyes are absorbed by the fibers of the wood to color it without creating a surface film. Nonpenetrating oil stains, also called pigmented wiping stains, contain pigments in suspension; these stains are thicker than the penetrating ones and deposit color on the wood fibers rather than soaking into them. In some cases, oil stains carry both dyes and pigments: If this is true of your stain, the top layer in the can will be transparent, but the bottom layer will be opaque; stir the two well and handle the mixture like a nonpenetrating stain (*opposite, bottom right*).

Stains based on solvents other than oil, although not widely available, are pigmented more subtly than either kind of oil stain. Among these are alcohol stains, sold either as powdered dye to be mixed with denatured alcohol (*opposite, top*) or as premixed liquids, and non-grain-raising (NGR) stains, which are based on a blend of solvents and sold only in liquid form. The NGR stains are prized because they are less likely to fade than other stains; they do not, of course, raise wood grain, but neither do modern oil and alcohol stains. Both alcohol and NGR stains are available from paint stores catering to the furniture-making trade.

Though not technically a stain, household ammonia can turn oak's amber color to driftwood gray by reacting with the wood's tannic acid. Simply sponge copious amounts of ammonia onto the wood.

For predictable results, always start by buying or mixing the smallest practical amount of stain so that you can test it. Test the stain on an unseen section of the furniture — the underside of a tabletop, for example — before staining prominent areas. Aim for a relatively light shade; it is much easier to darken stain by repeated applications than to lighten it.

If the wood in the test patch darkens excessively, switch to a lighter stain color or treat the wood with a sealer (*page 26*) to limit the stain's penetration. Or choose the kind of oil stain — called stain-sealer — that has a sealer built in.

Choosing the Right Stain

Category	Type	Common Brand	Recommended Use	Drying Time	Advantages	Disadvantages
Penetrating Stain	Denatured Alcohol	Behlen®	For woods with beautiful grain	15 minutes	Allows grain to show; does not raise grain; fast drying	Fades in sunlight after many years; overlaps show up as dark streaks; not widely available
	Non-grain-raising	Behlen®	For woods with beautiful grain	1 hour	Gives most transparent effect; does not fade; does not raise grain	Tends to show overlaps; not widely available
	Oil	Minwax®	For all woods	12-24 hours	Seals and stains in one step; flows and blends	Overemphasizes grain in some cases, giving zebra stripes or a candied look
Nonpenetrating Stain	Oil	Zar®	For woods with little or unattractive grain	12-24 hours	Obscures unattractive grain; gives appearance of uniform color	Gives opaque appearance; colors are not brilliant; does not cover well on hardwoods

Choosing stains. The function of a stain will guide its selection. As the chart above shows, each type of stain has advantages and disadvantages that make it appropriate to particular jobs. Drying times differ according to the kinds of solvent in the stains.

Quick Results from Alcohol Stain

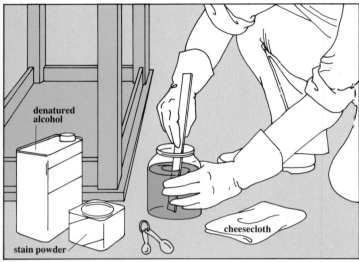

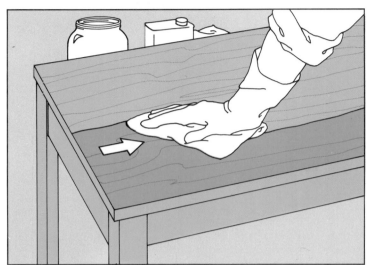

1 **Dissolving stain powder in alcohol.** Pour a quart of denatured alcohol into a plastic or glass container (not metal, which might be affected by the alcohol). Add 2 to 3 tablespoons of stain powder and stir until it dissolves. Use a folded cheesecloth pad to test the stain on an inconspicuous part of the furniture that is made of the featured wood — not a different, structural wood. When the test patch dries, adjust the color by adding powder to darken it or by diluting with alcohol to lighten it. Strain the stain through cheesecloth to remove undissolved powder.

2 **Applying the stain.** For uniform color, work on one area at a time. Wearing rubber gloves, dip the cheesecloth pad into the stain until it is damp but not dripping. Wipe on the stain in the direction of the grain. To avoid dark spots at overlaps, wipe stain along the still-wet edge of your last stroke. Then quickly wipe away excess stain with another pad. To lighten spots, rub denatured alcohol into the wood. Let the stain dry for at least 15 minutes. Build up the color by repeated applications, then let the stain dry for an hour before applying a finish.

A Slow-drying Oil Stain

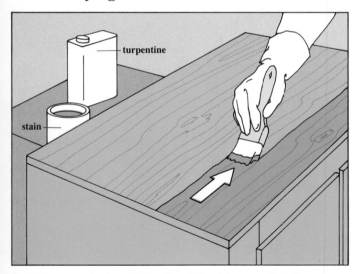

Brushing on penetrating oil stain. Brush the stain — undiluted — along the grain in even strokes. Darken the color as needed by applying more stain. At overlaps, wipe off excess stain with cheesecloth wetted with turpentine. Allow the first coat to dry for 12 hours before brushing on a second. Wait for 24 hours before applying a finish.

A Wipe-on, Wipe-off Oil Stain

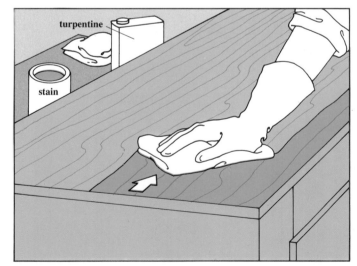

Wiping on nonpenetrating oil stain. Wearing rubber gloves, use cheesecloth to wipe the stain onto the wood in a thin coat. Wait until the stain has dulled, then wipe the excess off. Let the stain dry for 12 to 24 hours, or until it feels dry to the touch. Repeat the application if the stain is not dark enough. Warning: Do not let the stain dry without wiping it. The excess will form an ugly, opaque coating that will have to be removed with turpentine.

Distressing wood to mimic aging

Distressing — the technique of making new furniture look old by damaging it intentionally — will be most effective if you exercise restraint. Too much damage, placed indiscriminately, looks artificial — even junky. For a convincing antique look, base your distressing on the kinds of minor dents, nicks and scratches that would have occurred over decades or centuries to well-kept furniture.

The best time to distress a piece is when the wood is raw or newly stripped. Study the object carefully and work out a plan for where to put what kinds of marks. Edges and corners are a good place to start. These become rounded slightly over the years from dusting and polishing; such wear can be imitated by blunting edges with the flat side of a file.

The back of a chair gathers scratches when it is pushed repeatedly against a wall. You can achieve the same effect by scribing the wood with the tip of a nail.

The rung of an old chair will bear the marks of countless shoes and boots, as will table legs that have been kicked frequently. You can put a long groove in a chair rung by scraping it with the rounded side of a file. To nick a table's top or one of its legs, strike it two or three times with a bunch of keys.

The table shown here both before distressing *(below)* and after *(right)* illustrates the effects of the methods demonstrated opposite and suggests the proper lengths to which you should carry this kind of damage.

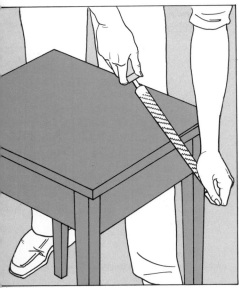

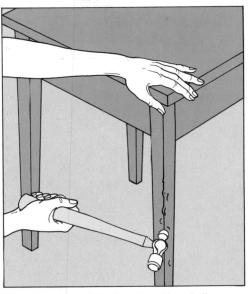

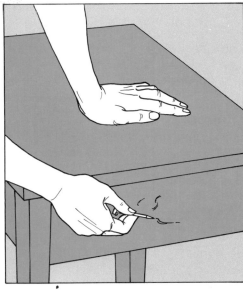

1 **Rounding edges.** Hold a 10-inch, half-round smooth file flat side down over one edge of a tabletop, as shown above. Push the file downward and away from you repeatedly to round the edge slightly. Work along the edge to the corner, then along each of the other edges in turn. Sand the distressed areas first with medium (100-grit) sandpaper, then with fine (150-grit) sandpaper and finally with very-fine (220-grit) sandpaper.

2 **Blunting and denting edges.** Use a ball-peen hammer and strike lightly near the middle of one edge and the adjacent sides of the lower part of a table leg. Overlap the blows to conceal the kind of tool employed. Repeat near the bottom of another table leg. Then strike several blows on the bottom edge of the table's skirt to form a dent there. Sand the distressed areas.

3 **Scratching.** Grip a tenpenny (3-inch) common nail between your thumb and first two fingers. Scribe short, irregular scratches into the vertical skirt panels under the table-top. Sand the distressed areas.

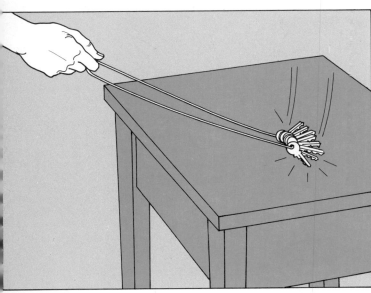

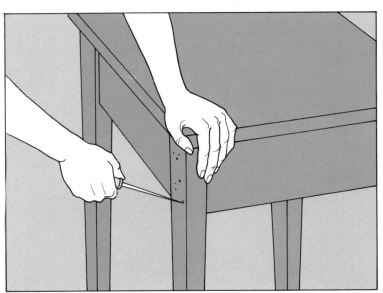

4 **Scarring.** String eight or 10 keys on a 2-foot cord, and tie the ends of the cord together. Grasp the cord and swing the keys up above your shoulder, then let them fall onto the table. Repeat two or three times to create an irregular pattern of dents. Sand the distressed areas.

5 **Imitating wormholes.** Holding an awl by its handle, twist the point about 1/16 inch into the wood. Then untwist the awl to leave a smooth tunnel like the one a woodworm-beetle grub makes by feeding on wood. Put small clusters of five or six holes each in three places, two clusters on a leg and one near the edge of the tabletop. Sand the distressed areas.

What to do with an old finish

How you prepare an old piece of furniture for refinishing depends on the condition of the existing finish and what kind of new finish you plan to apply.

If the old finish is not badly bubbled or cracked and if the new one will be opaque — paint, enamel, colored lacquer — preparations are minimal. First, wipe grease and dirt off the piece of furniture with a cloth dipped in warm water mixed with a mild detergent. Wring out the cloth before using it on the furniture, so that water does not seep into pores and cracks, raising the wood's grain. Then fill any cracks or gouges with wood putty *(page 25)*. Finally, sand the entire piece lightly with fine (150-grit) sandpaper to roughen the surface slightly, giving it a "tooth" to which the new finish will adhere.

If the existing finish is too badly damaged to paint over, or if you plan to apply a new, clear finish, the old finish must be entirely removed. This process, called stripping, consists of softening the old finish with a paint-and-varnish remover, then lifting it off the surface to expose the bare wood underneath.

The best all-purpose furniture strippers for home use are solutions containing methylene chloride. These act by chemically dissolving the old finish. Caustic soda and oxalic acid are other all-purpose strippers, but they are harmful to the skin and difficult to work with; trisodium phosphate, methyl alcohol and lacquer thinner work well only on specific types of finish. Methylene chloride strippers come in a semipaste form that has the consistency of molasses and in a thinner, liquid form. The semipastes are the easiest to use because they cling to vertical surfaces and evaporate slowly, giving the chemicals ample time to work.

All strippers require temperatures of at least 70° F. in order for their chemical agents to react with the finish. Because these agents can irritate your skin and lungs, it is best to work outdoors. If you must work indoors, put an exhaust fan i[n] the window and keep the furniture be[-] tween you and the fan so fumes will b[e] drawn away from you. Always wear pro[-] tective rubber gloves and goggles whe[n] working with stripper.

Before you begin stripping, remove al[l] drawers, doors, hardware, glass and mir[-] rors from the furniture. Start with on[e] well-defined area, such as a tabletop or [a] chair seat, and strip it completely befor[e] moving on to another section. Never al[-] low the stripper to dry before lifting it of[f] the furniture with a putty knife *(opposite[,] Step 2):* It will harden and become diff[i-] cult to remove.

Many old pieces of furniture have bee[n] painted repeatedly over the years, an[d] the first application of stripper may no[t] remove all the old finishes. Be patient[.] Strippers usually take off only one lay[-] er of paint or varnish at a time. Jus[t] repeat the procedure to expose and re[-] move successive layers until you ge[t] down to bare wood.

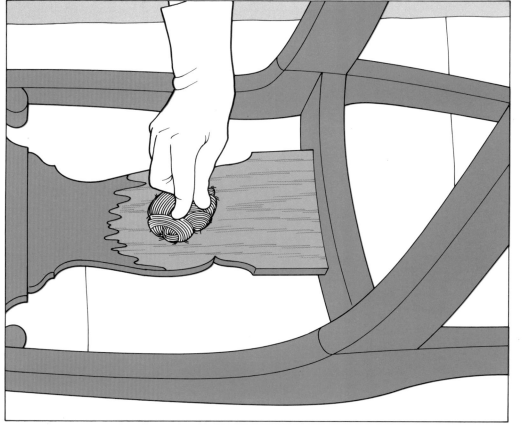

3 **Smoothing the surface.** Still wearing rubber gloves, unroll a pad of medium (1/0 or 2/0) steel wool and tear off a small section. Working with the grain, use the steel wool to gently scrub the area you have just stripped until it is smooth and free of all finish. Then apply remover to another small section of a flat surface, turning the piece of furniture if necessary, and strip off the finish similarly. Finally, strip the finish from such smaller elements as legs, arms, turnings and carvings.

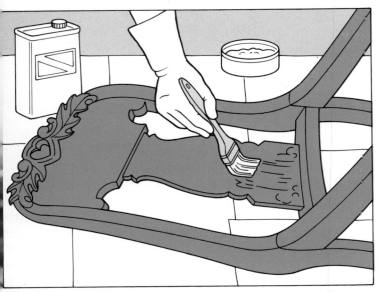

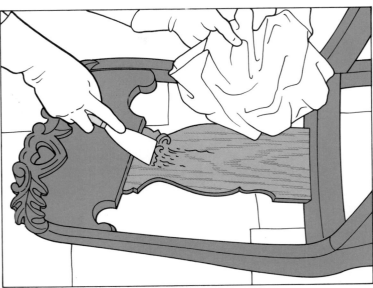

1 **Applying the stripper.** Place the piece of furniture on a work surface covered with old newspaper. Wearing rubber gloves, pour a little stripper into a shallow metal or glass container. Then, starting with a horizontal surface, pat the stripper evenly onto a small section of the furniture with an old paintbrush. Let the stripper stand until visible bubbles in the finish indicate it is softening, usually after about 10 to 15 minutes.

2 **Lifting off the old finish.** Slide the blade of a 3-inch putty knife across the surface of the furniture in short, light strokes parallel to the grain to lift up the old finish and the remover. As you proceed, wipe the putty knife with a wad of crumpled newspaper. If some parts of the finish do not come up easily, do not try to scrape them off, lest you damage the wood; apply a second coat of remover, wait five to 10 minutes and try lifting the finish with the putty knife again. When the area has been stripped, use a soft cloth or a piece of terry cloth to wipe away any remnants of remover or dissolved finish from the surface. Working with the grain, rub the wood vigorously until it is dry.

4 **Detailing contours and carvings.** Run the tip of a penknife and then — if need be — an awl along contour lines and inside carvings to lift out the last bits of old finish and remover. Work gently: The wood may have been softened by the stripper and could easily be gouged. Brush away any residue with a small wire-bristle brush or an old toothbrush. Finally, sand the whole piece lightly with very-fine (220-grit) paper. To restore a uniform color tone to the wood, concentrate your sanding on areas that have been discolored by the old finish.

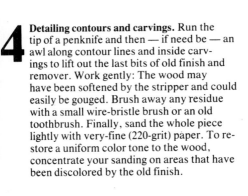

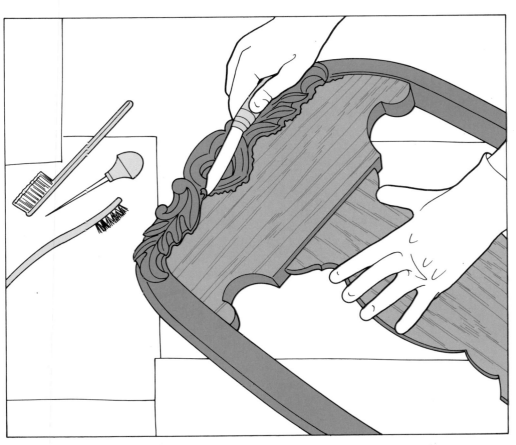

A repertoire of basic finishes

Dramatic transformations take place when a finish is applied to furniture. Suddenly a prized heirloom regains its original luster. A scruffy discard rebounds, its mars and stains concealed beneath a bright coat of color. Or a raw new purchase assumes the subtle character of a seasoned antique.

As its name implies, a finish is the final material to be applied to a furniture surface. The maple spheres at right demonstrate what effects can be achieved with finishes ranging from oils, which leave the grain not only visible but palpable, to enamels, which obscure the surface with an opaque colored film.

Besides varying in appearance, finishes also differ in the amount and kind of protection they provide and in the ease with which they can be applied. Deciding which finish to use depends on how much wear a piece of furniture will receive and how much time and skill you bring to the undertaking. The chart on pages 38-39 is designed to help you make a wise selection.

Among the many types of finishes, the chief distinction is between those that soak into the fibers of the wood and those that develop a hard film on top of it. A surface finish forms an obvious protective shield; a penetrating oil works more subtly by combining with the subsurface fibers and hardening them as it dries. This helps the wood ward off damage from abrasion, dirt and moisture.

The best-known of the oil finishes is boiled linseed oil *(page 40)*. Linseed-oil products are rubbed into the wood time and again until the wood is completely saturated. But a similar appearance can be obtained with a good deal less effort by the use of heat-treated tung oil, a fast-drying finish that forms a hard, water-resistant film, prized since antiquity in China. Also available are modern oil finishes that require only three applications: These finishes are known by such names as teak oil, Danish oil and Swedish oil, because they were originally associated with Scandinavian furniture *(page 40)*.

Surface finishes — shellac, lacquer, varnish, enamel and paint — are based on resins and volatile solvents, and often contain oils. The resins and oils form the hard surface film that remains after the volatile solvents evaporate. In shellac, for example, natural resin is dissolved in alcohol to produce a liquid; the resin creates a coating when the liquid dries.

Lacquer is based on nitrocellulose and includes resins and plasticizers dissolved in organic solvents *(page 48)*. Varnishes and enamels *(pages 44-47)* incorporate natural and synthetic resins combined by heat with vegetable oils. They also contain driers and volatile solvents. Latex enamels and paints are emulsions rather than solutions, as are oil-based varnishes and enamels. The resins they contain are dispersed, or emulsified, in water.

The traditional solvent for varnishes and enamels was turpentine, but in modern preparations it is more likely to be mineral spirits — a distilled petroleum-based product. Similarly, sunflower, safflower, castor and soy-bean oils often replace or supplement the once-customary linseed oil or tung oil.

Although most varnishes and enamels contain more than one resin and oil, they are often classified by the principal resin they contain. In the types suitable for furniture, four resins are commonly used. Two, polyurethane and epoxy, produce surfaces that are highly durable and resistant to water and abrasion. Acrylic resins are remarkable for their crystalline clarity and their resistance to yellowing. Alkyd resins, which are often blended with other resins, are notable for being easy to use.

Varnishes and enamels also contain metallic salts that speed the drying process. Nonetheless, the most important other ingredient is pigment. The presence of pigments that give color and opacity is the principal difference between an enamel and a varnish. And the fine grind of its pigments is one of the chief characteristics that distinguish an enamel from other paints.

Even varnishes may contain pigments, since it is the addition of inert, transparent pigments, called flatteners, that cause a varnish, enamel or paint to dry to a flat, satin or semigloss finish instead of a glossy one. The list of ingredients that appears on most cans of enamel and paint will detail the pigments separately, while other elements — resin, solvent, oil, drier and plasticizer — will be grouped together under the term "vehicle."

A sampler of finishing effects. The spheres — actually, drawer knobs — at right illustrate how different finishes vary in effect. All of the knobs are maple; all began as unfinished wood. The top left-hand knob was treated only with penetrating oil; three coats produced the finish shown. All of the other knobs were sealed with orange shellac, then given three coats of the finish specified. Varnishes with increasing amounts of flatting pigment have successively less gloss, whereas increasing the amounts of resins in enamels adds to their shininess.

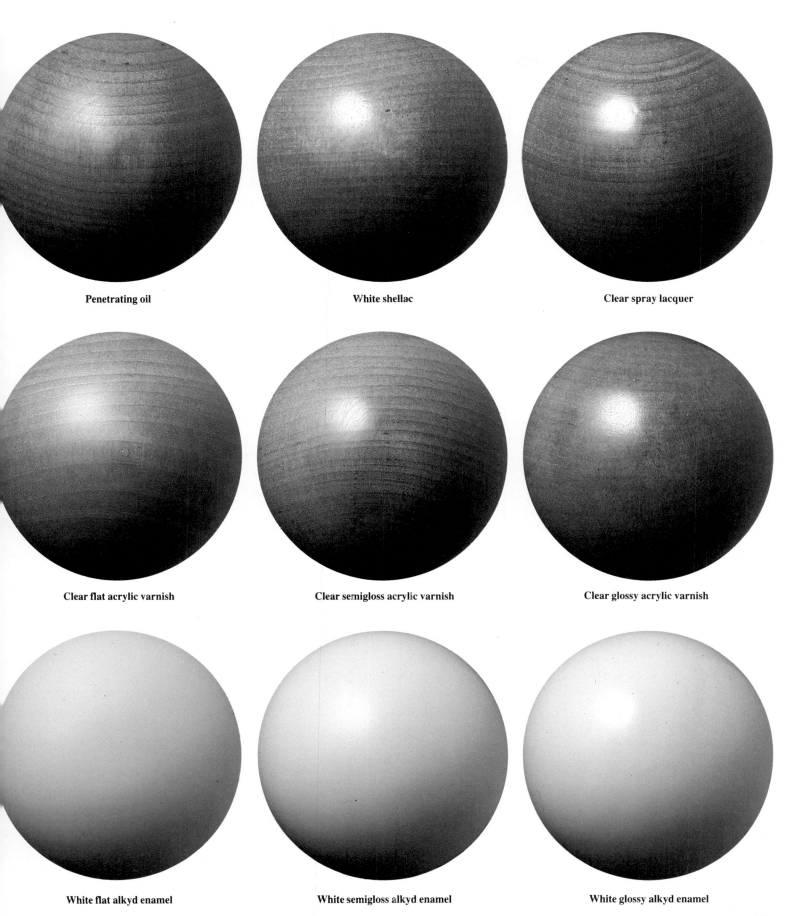

Penetrating oil

White shellac

Clear spray lacquer

Clear flat acrylic varnish

Clear semigloss acrylic varnish

Clear glossy acrylic varnish

White flat alkyd enamel

White semigloss alkyd enamel

White glossy alkyd enamel

Choosing the right product

Endlessly varied as the furniture finishes available from paint dealers seem to be, most belong to one or another of the types shown in the chart at right. For each type, the chart gives the basic ingredients, the common variations of its form, its fundamental characteristics and the advantages and disadvantages it presents. Demonstrations of how to apply the different types begin on page 40.

Finishes are not standardized, of course. Manufacturers use basic ingredients in different ratios and augment them with additives for improving durability, shelf life, drying time, clarity and spreadability. When in doubt about a product, look for an ingredients list on the back of the can and for the manufacturer's suggestions about the product's applications. And consult the dealer. A reputable one should be well informed and able to advise you on your selection.

In most cases, the ingredients of finishes separate to some degree during storage. The dealer will give the can a vigorous shake by machine when he sells it. Then, if you use the finish within a few days, simply stir it with a mixing paddle before applying it.

However, if you have kept an enamel for some time, the pigment may have settled to the bottom of the can. You can quickly return the enamel to its original condition by using a stirrer attachment for a variable-speed drill. Another method is to pour the enamel back and forth from the can to a second container — a paper paint bucket available from the paint dealer, for example — stirring all the while to blend the ingredients.

A Chart of Comparative Qualities

Finish	Basic ingredients	Variations
Penetrating Oil	Boiled linseed oil, heat-treated tung oil or other vegetable oil.	Oils may be blended, heat-treated and combined with resins and varnishes.
Shellac	A natural resin — produced by the Asian insect *laccifer lacca* — dissolved in denatured alcohol.	Used in its natural reddish brown state, the resin yields orange shellac; when bleached, it yields white shellac. The thickness of shellac solutions varies with the ratio of shellac to alcohol.
Lacquer	Nitrocellulose, resins such as alkyd, solvents and plasticizers. For colored lacquer, pigments.	Clear or in a wide array of colors.
Acrylic Varnish	Acrylic resins dissolved in fast-evaporating solvents.	Available in flat, semigloss and glossy lusters.
Alkyd Varnish	Alkyd resins, vegetable oils, solvents and driers.	Available in flat, semigloss and glossy lusters. Exterior grades available for outdoor furniture.
Epoxy Varnish	Epoxy resins combined with oils, solvents and driers.	Available in flat, semigloss and glossy lusters.
Two-Part Epoxy Clear Coating	One component contains epoxy resin and solvents, while the other contains an agent that causes hardening when the two parts are mixed. The label directions must be followed carefully.	Available in semigloss and glossy lusters.
Polyurethane Varnish	Polyurethane (urethane) resins combined with oils, solvents and driers.	Available in flat, semigloss and glossy lusters. Exterior grades available for outdoor furniture.
Acrylic Enamel	Acrylic resins dissolved in fast-evaporating solvents, combined with colored pigments.	Available in flat, semigloss and glossy lusters, and in a wide array of colors.
Acrylic Latex Enamel	Polymerized acrylic resins emulsified with water; oils or other resins may be included.	Available in flat, semigloss and glossy lusters, and in a wide array of colors.
Alkyd Enamel	Alkyd resins combined with oils, solvents, driers and colored pigments.	Available in flat, semigloss and glossy lusters, and in a wide array of colors. Exterior grades available for outdoor furniture.
Epoxy Enamel	Epoxy resins combined with oils, solvents, driers and colored pigments.	Available glossy in a limited range of colors.
Two-Part Epoxy Enamel	One component contains epoxy resins and solvents, while the other contains colored pigments and an agent that causes hardening when the two parts are mixed. The label directions must be followed carefully.	Available glossy in a limited range of colors.
Polyurethane Enamel	Polyurethane (urethane) resins combined with oils, solvents, driers and colored pigments.	Available in flat, semigloss and glossy lusters, and in a wide array of colors. Exterior grades available for outdoor furniture.

aracteristics	Advantages	Disadvantages
oduces a luster and, with frequent olications, a thin film.	Easy to apply with good results; easily repaired.	Dries slowly. Not resistant to water or alcohol. Requires waxing for durability.
oduces a hard, transparent film. Orange ellac gives wood a distinctive amber hue; ite shellac is practically colorless.	Brushes on smoothly when thin; dries quickly; sands easily. A good wood sealer.	Difficult to brush on when thick. Many coats are necessary to give durability. Not resistant to water or alcohol. A top coat of wax is recommended to protect the surface. Loses its drying ability when stored a long time.
oduces a thin, hard film of exceptional rity.	Dries rapidly. Provides excellent resistance to wear and spills.	Quick drying can make it hard to apply except with a spray can or spray gun. Should not be applied over other finishes, as solvents may soften and wrinkle old finish. Lacquer is highly volatile; work in a well-ventilated space away from pilot lights and other ignition sources.
oduces a hard film that is notable for being stal clear with no hint of amber.	Allows the true color of woods to show through and does not yellow with time or sun exposure. Dries quickly.	Because it dries quickly, acrylic varnish may be hard to apply unless sprayed on. Only moderately resistant to wear and spills.
oduces a hard, transparent film that darkens ods slightly.	Easy to apply with predictably good results. Suitable for all but the most heavily used surfaces.	Only moderately resistant to wear and spills.
oduces a hard, transparent film that darkens ods slightly.	Excellent resistance to wear and spills. Adheres well to many materials besides woods — metals, for example.	Darkens with age. Hardness of the surface makes sanding difficult; follow label directions carefully.
oduces a thick, clear, plastic-like film.	Exceptionally tough and resistant to wear and spills.	Two-part epoxy contains volatile solvents; work in a well-ventilated space away from pilot lights and other ignition sources that can spark a fire. Gives furniture the appearance of being encased in plastic.
oduces a hard, transparent film that darkens ods slightly.	Excellent resistance to wear and spills. Easy to apply with good results.	Darkens with age. Hardness of the surface makes sanding difficult; to avoid sanding between coats, apply the subsequent coat within the drying time specified on the label. May not be suitable for use over shellac.
oduces a hard, opaque film that is notable, ecially in light colors, for not having an ber hue.	Colors resist darkening with age. Provides the whitest whites and truest pale colors of all enamels. Does not yellow with time or sun exposure.	Dries quickly and may be tricky to apply unless sprayed on. Only moderately resistant to wear and spills.
oduces a firm, opaque film.	Easy to apply with good results; cleans up easily. Nonflammable.	To avoid raising the wood's grain, apply only after sealing the wood with shellac or an enamel undercoat. Moderate resistance to wear and spills.
oduces a hard, opaque film.	Easy to apply with good results. Suitable for all but the most heavily used furniture.	Only moderately resistant to wear and spills.
oduces an exceptionally hard, opaque film.	Excellent resistance to wear and spills. Adheres to metals as well as wood	May darken with age. Hardness of the surface makes producing a rubbed finish difficult; follow label directions carefully.
oduces a thick, opaque, plastic-like film.	Long wearing. Exceptional resistance to wear and spills — even mild acids and alkalis.	Gives furniture the appearance of being encased in plastic. Two-part epoxy contains volatile solvents; work in a well-ventilated space away from pilot lights and other ignition sources that can spark a fire.
oduces an exceptionally hard, opaque film.	Excellent resistance to wear and spills.	May darken with age. Hardness of the surface makes producing a rubbed finish difficult; to avoid sanding between coats, apply the subsequent coat within the drying time specified on the label. Test before using over shellac.

Easy protection with penetrating oils

Few finishes are as easy to apply and maintain as penetrating oil. The oil flows smoothly when brushed on or spread with a cloth; after it dries, it requires only buffing to complete the process. Once applied, an oil finish helps to protect the surface of the wood against moisture, dirt and stains, while enhancing the wood's grain pattern and its color.

An oil finish will neither chip nor peel and, though not as durable as varnish, it can be maintained with a fresh coat every year or so; between times minor stains or scratches in the finish can be rubbed out with fine steel wool and covered with a bit of added oil.

On the other hand, oils make wood darker and tend to blotch softwoods — such as pine, poplar and gum. If the wood color must be stable, choose a finish without linseed oil, which darkens with age. Before making a final selection of a penetrating oil, test it on an unobtrusive patch of furniture; be sure that your sample section is made of the same wood as the section you intend to finish.

Penetrating-oil products come in two types: those with little or no resin, which leave very little surface film when they dry, and those with a resin content high enough to form a film and yield a hard, thin surface coat.

The low-resin group includes teak oil and Danish oil. These oils create a subtle, satin finish. The grain pattern can be seen and felt, and the natural color of the wood is intensified, as the sideboard below illustrates.

High-resin penetrating oils may contain heat-treated tung oil, boiled linseed oil, some kind of varnish and/or synthetic resins. When applied repeatedly these oils build up into a durable, lustrous coating similar to — although not quite so shiny or hard as — shellac or varnish. Because these oils solidify within the cells of the wood, they enhance the wood's resistance to dents and scratches.

All penetrating-oil products are applied in essentially the same manner, although manufacturers' recommendations may vary slightly because of differences in the proprietary formulas.

Always follow the directions for the product you select. Penetrating oils can be applied over stains, but not over integral finishes such as varnish or lacquer, which would prevent the oil from penetrating the wood.

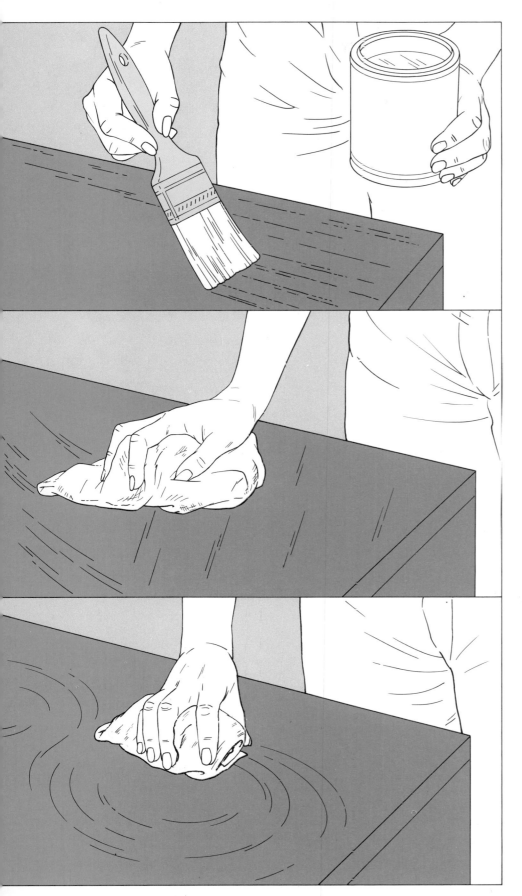

1 **Applying oil.** Set the piece of furniture in a well-ventilated, dust-free area. Remove drawers, doors and hardware as necessary. To make sure that the furniture is completely clear of dust, wipe the surface with a soft, lint-free cloth. Using a brush or lint-free cloth, spread the oil liberally over one surface at a time. After 15 minutes or so, reapply the oil to any sections where the oil has been completely absorbed and the surface is dry. Wait for another 15 minutes, then wipe off all of the oil with a clean, soft cloth. Caution: As oil-soaked cloth dries out, it may ignite spontaneously. Wet the cloth thoroughly with water and dispose of it in a metal trash container.

2 **Polishing the finish.** Let the oil dry for at least 24 hours — longer if high humidity or low temperature slows the drying process. Rub the surface with extra-fine (3/0) steel wool — working always with the grain. Wipe off the surface with a cloth, then apply another coat of the oil; repeat if necessary to build up the desired sheen. When the final coat is dry, use a clean, soft cloth to buff it vigorously — in a circular motion. The heat generated by the rubbing slightly softens resins and oils so that the finish can be further smoothed.

3 **Adding luster.** To impart an extra-smooth finish, lubricate the finest (4/0) steel wool with a small amount of lemon oil. Using light strokes, rub the wood along its grain with the steel wool. Wipe off the oil from the furniture and allow the surface to dry; then polish it by buffing in a circular motion with a clean cloth.

Shellac for a fast, clear shine

Shellac imparts a transparent, glasslike luster to furniture, yet it is among the easiest finishes to apply. Basically, shellac is a natural resin dissolved in denatured alcohol. The resin comes from Asia, from deposits exuded onto tree twigs and branches by the tiny lac bug.

Two types of shellac are commonly available: orange, which is the natural color of the resin and imparts a warm tint to wood; and white, which is made by bleaching orange shellac and creates a colorless clear finish. Both produce a hard surface, but orange shellac is slightly more elastic and thus a bit more durable.

Dry shellac resin — which comes as flakes or the pellets known as buttons — is available where furniture-making supplies are sold. Dissolved lac resin is sold in most paint stores. The proportion of resin to alcohol in the solution is called its cut. The resin is traditionally measured in pounds, the alcohol in gallons. Thus a 4-pound cut means that there are 4 pounds of resin to each gallon of alcohol; most shellac is a 4-pound or 5-pound cut.

Because a 4-pound or 5-pound cut forms a relatively thick coat, the shellac can be difficult to spread evenly without runs, brush marks or other imperfections. Instead of applying one thick coat, thin the shellac to a 1-pound cut, use three or four coats, and sand between them. To make a 1-pound cut, mix three parts of denatured alcohol with one part of 4-pound-cut shellac, or four parts of alcohol with one part of 5-pound-cut shellac.

Choose a workplace that has good ventilation and low humidity: The alcohol is highly flammable, and moving air is needed to disperse its fumes. High humidity can cloud the finish as you apply it; the moisture condensing on the surface can break the lac resin out of solution.

To ensure the quickest application, use the largest brush convenient for the surface — a 2- or 3-inch-wide brush for broad areas, 1- or 2-inch-wide brushes for legs and rungs. Clean your brushes with denatured alcohol between coats.

After the last coat has been applied and smoothed, give the shellac finish a sturdy coating of paste wax to protect it from water and other liquids. With occasional waxing, a shellac finish can last for a long time. Just be sure to keep it away from liquids and sources of intense heat, which can cause the surface to blister.

French Polish: A Time-honored Technique

Despite its name, French polish is not a special waxen top coat, but a shellac-based finish developed by European violin makers and furniture finishers to produce an exceptionally brilliant, transparent finish.

Although the original French polishing techniques are still secret, a modern strategy can produce the same kind of effects:

The finish is applied with a thick cloth pad, made by covering several folded layers of an absorbent material such as muslin with a layer of soft, lint-free cotton or linen. The pad is wetted with a mixture of thin shellac — a 1-pound cut, for example — and boiled linseed oil, in a ratio of 8 ounces of shellac to ½ teaspoon of oil. Next, the pad is rubbed across the surface with a circular motion, working from the center out to the edges. The linseed oil lubricates the pad so that the shellac layer is very smooth.

Each coat is allowed to dry for approximately an hour, then is burnished with very-fine steel wool before more shellac is applied, building up to a total of at least eight coats.

When the finish has reached the desired thickness, a pad with only a little shellac is moistened with denatured alcohol and rubbed over the surface with a circular motion to remove excess oil.

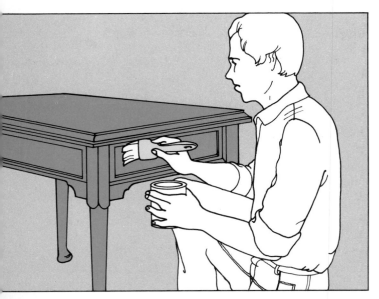

1 **Applying the shellac.** Dip a soft-bristle brush two thirds of the way into the shellac; the bristles should be saturated, but not dripping. Working on one section at a time, flow shellac onto the vertical planes and turnings with light strokes along the grain. Brush only in one direction on each surface, and lift the brush away from the surface at the end of each stroke. Where strokes overlap, brush from the bare surface onto the covered surface, then lift the brush. Brush slowly to avoid bubbles.

2 **Applying additional coats.** Cover all of the vertical surfaces, then flow shellac onto the horizontal surfaces. Allow the first coat to dry to a hard finish — at least four hours — then sand it with very-fine (220-grit) sandpaper. Wipe the surface clean. Apply a second and third coat of shellac in the same manner, sanding between coats. Smooth the final coat with the finest (4/0) steel wool, rubbing in the direction of the grain.

3 **Waxing the surface.** Use a pad of 4/0 steel wool to apply a coat of furniture paste wax to the dried shellac. Keep a generous amount of wax on the pad and rub it on in the direction of the grain. Allow the wax to dry according to the manufacturer's directions — usually about 30 minutes.

4 **Buffing the wax.** Attach a lamb's-wool buffing pad to a power drill, and use it to polish the wax on flat surfaces, moving the pad slowly in the direction of the grain while maintaining light pressure. To buff inside corners and carved areas and along legs, fold a clean, soft cloth into a small pad and polish by hand, using light pressure and a circular motion.

Hard-wearing varnish

Varnish forms a tough, clear finish that protects wood from water, abrasion and hot objects, while allowing its natural beauty to shine through. This happy combination of qualities makes varnish ideal for furniture that gets hard use, such as the butler's tray table below. This table was bought unfinished, then was stained, sealed with white shellac (to keep the stain from reacting with the varnish) and given two coats of clear alkyd varnish. Here the varnish was low gloss, or satin finish; glossy or flat lusters would serve as well, but should also be clear. Stain is a more controllable coloring agent for the wood than dye-tinted varnish.

Modern varnishes are made from a variety of synthetic resins (chart, pages 38-39). Choose a product recommended for furniture, and read the instructions for special precautions; for example, some polyurethane varnishes should not be applied over a shellac sealer.

Successful varnishing begins before you open the can. First, remove the furniture's hardware. Take out drawers and remove doors or, as here, the drop leaves of the table. Clean off dirt and grease with a clean rag lightly moistened in mineral spirits, then gently sand rough spots with very-fine (220-grit) sandpaper.

Dust specks invisible in the air seem to loom like mountains when they land on a pristine plane of sticky varnish. Sweep or vacuum the workroom thoroughly, and dust all horizontal surfaces. Damp-mop the floor to hold down dust. If possible, place the furniture on a worktable to bring it to eye level. Wipe the piece to be varnished with a clean, lint-free cloth, or vacuum it with a brush attachment. Finally, go over the piece with a tack rag (page 47) to pick up minute particles.

Varnish may be applied with a spray gun (pages 50-51), but it more commonly is put on with a brush. Use only new, chisel-cut varnish brushes: a 2-inch-wide brush for broad surfaces and a 1-inch-wide brush for narrower surfaces, tight corners and legs. Besides the varnish itself, you need only super-fine (400-grit) sandpaper. Pour only the amount of varnish needed for the day's work into a clean, wide-mouthed jar or can; reseal the remainder tightly. To prevent bubbles in the coating, do not shake the varnish. Just stir it gently with a clean stick. After varnishing, discard the contents of the container; do not return it to the original can lest it contain dust or other contaminants.

To develop an understanding of how varnish flows, practice brushstrokes on a scrap board or an inconspicuous area of the furniture. Brush the varnish onto the furniture one section at a time, as demonstrated here. Let the varnish dry thoroughly according to the manufacturer's instructions — usually 24 hours — before applying successive coats; be sure to recoat polyurethane varnish within the time specified. Between coats, wrap brushes in aluminum foil or clear plastic wrap and store them in the freezer, or suspend the bristles in mineral spirits.

Smooth each coat with super-fine (400-grit) wet-and-dry sandpaper (page 22). Apply two coats of varnish over a sealer or previous finish; over bare or stained wood, use at least three coats. For a satiny luster, smooth the surface with rubbing compound, then apply paste wax. If you are using a high-gloss varnish, do not sand or rub the final coat.

1 **Coating cross braces and legs.** Detach drop leaves from the table and put them aside. Set the table at a convenient height. Pour varnish into a wide-mouthed jar to a depth of 3 or 4 inches. Dip the bristles of a 1-inch brush about halfway into the varnish. Do not wipe the bristles across the rim of the jar; instead, gently press the bristles against the inside walls of the jar to remove excess varnish. Coat one surface of the cross braces at a time with light strokes along its length. Do not allow the bristles to flop over the edges and mar the adjacent sides, and do not wipe the brush across an edge — it will leave a drip. Next, varnish the legs one by one, applying the varnish in a thin coat so that it will not run.

2 **Varnishing the skirt.** Dip the brush in varnish, squeeze out the excess and gently push the bristles against the end of one skirt panel where it meets the leg. Brush toward the center of the skirt in short strokes; leave only a thin coat to prevent having the varnish drip. Reload the brush as needed. Stop at the center of the skirt, then begin from the opposite end. At the center, bring the strokes up to — but not over — the first set of strokes by lifting the brush as you complete each one. Finally, smooth the panel by making several strokes from end to end, barely touching the varnish surface with the tips of nearly dry bristles.

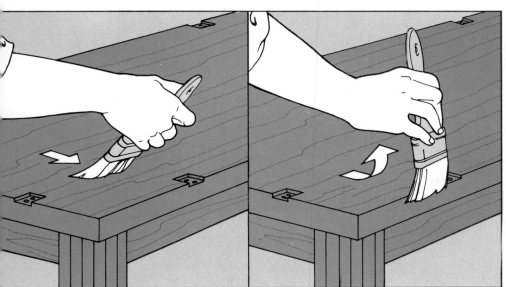

3 **Applying varnish to the tabletop.** Dip a 2-inch brush halfway into the varnish; do not squeeze out the excess. Holding the handle like a pencil, lay the bristles on the tabletop and brush across the grain *(above, left)*. Apply the varnish in side-by-side strokes, or use separated strokes and go back to fill in the spaces. At an edge, lift the bristles *(above, right)* to avoid creating a ridge of varnish. When the entire surface is coated, use an almost-dry brush to smooth the varnish in long, light strokes with the grain. Varnish the tabletop edges with a 1-inch brush. Work from the ends toward the center of each edge, taking care not to mar the tabletop. Then varnish the bottom and edge of each drop leaf; when the varnish has dried — after about 24 hours — varnish the tops of the leaves.

4 **Sanding between coats.** Insert super-fine (400-grit) sandpaper in a sanding block *(page 23)*. Stroke with the grain, using just enough pressure to dull the sheen. Use special care so as not to sand through the varnish to bare wood. Abrade areas that a sanding block cannot reach with the finest (4/0) steel wool. Wipe off the residue with a clean cloth.

A benefaction of color from enamels and paints

Painted finishes figure in many furniture styles — Chippendale, Louis XIV, Pennsylvania Dutch and Art Deco among them. The past and present popularity of such finishes is easy to understand: Paint offers the freedom to select a color that complements a piece of furniture, suits a particular setting or carries out a decorating scheme.

Just about any color can be achieved in paints, which run the gamut from glossy to flat. The bold blue of the child's table and chairs below, for example, glistens bright. On the other hand, the muted green and coral of the corner cupboard at right have only a hint of luster.

Paints can serve practical as well as esthetic purposes. They cover undistin-guished woods and grain patterns. And they mask putty and other repairs.

In a broad sense, the term "paint" applies to any material composed of solid coloring agents dispersed in liquid that dries to create an opaque film; technically, enamels are differentiated from paints — chiefly because the color pigments in enamels are ground somewhat finer. Both paints and enamels are available in oil-based (solvent-thinned) and latex (water-thinned) types *(chart, pages 38-39)*. Enamels, which dry to a smoother and generally harder film than paints, are the wiser choice for furniture.

In oil-based enamels, the resins and oils that determine durability are often the same as those in varnish. A polyure-thane or epoxy enamel is best for a heavi-ly used chair or table, whereas an alkyd enamel will do just fine on a bookcase.

The preparations of the wood for oil-based enamel are the same as for varnish. Set the piece in a dust-free work space. Take off the hardware and removable parts such as doors, drawers, shelves and mirrors. Wipe off dirt and grease with a rag moistened in mineral spirits; use a tack rag *(box, below)* to pick up fine dust.

With raw hardwood or stripped wood, start by sanding it smooth *(pages 22-23)* and applying an enamel undercoat, following the techniques for varnish *(page 44-45)*. Put on the undercoat and later the enamel with clean chisel-cut varnish brushes — a 2-inch brush for wide, flat surfaces and a smaller one for turnings, tight corners and edges. Let the under

oat dry thoroughly — 18 to 24 hours. and the surface smooth with super-fine 400-grit) paper, then enamel it. Three oats, the first two followed by sanding, re generally enough.

With softwoods such as fir or pine, first wipe knots and other resinous areas with denatured alcohol. Seal the wood with hellac *(pages 42-43)* before applying layers of enamel undercoat and enamel.

Latex-based enamels, while not as ough as oil-based enamels, can be applied considerably faster. Raw hardwood or stripped wood must first receive a latex undercoat; softwood needs to be shelacked before it is primed. The job can be inished in short order. Latex products low on smoothly, leaving a minimum of rush marks, and they can be applied to road surfaces with 3-inch or 4-inch rushes. They dry quickly, so several oats could be put on in one day, although wo coats are usually ample.

Both latex and oil-based paints sometimes serve as furniture finishes, even though they are less slick and hardy than namel. Paints may provide colors not vailable in enamels; or they may serve to match built-in furniture to the wall behind t. Paints also furnish the faintly rough ase needed for acrylic stencil paints *pages 56-60)*. Painted furniture is often iven a protective coat of varnish to increase the wearability of the finish.

Making a Tack Rag

A so-called tack rag is a furniture finisher's stand-by. Its sticky, or tacky, surface makes it possible to wipe up the tiniest dust particles.

Although tack rags are sold by paint stores, they are simple and inexpensive to produce at home: Dip a cheesecloth in warm water, and wring it well. Then saturate the cloth with turpentine and shake it out. Drip varnish evenly over the cloth, fold it up and knead it until the varnish is spread uniformly; the cloth should feel sticky, but not wet. Store the rag in a sealed container. To rejuvenate it, periodically add more turpentine and water.

Luster from a lacquer spray

Only lacquer gives the smooth, deeply lustrous finish seen on the table below. Yet this luminous look does not require hours of labor; lacquer can be sprayed on from an aerosol can.

Lacquer has other advantages. It dries so rapidly that a second coat can be added after 20 minutes. It can be rubbed or polished to almost any degree of gloss. And it forms an extremely durable finish.

But spraying lacquer requires special precautions. Lacquer is highly flammable and emits noxious fumes. Spray outdoors or in a well-ventilated room, and wear a respirator that filters out fumes. Extinguish all flames, including pilot lights, and allow no lighted cigarettes. Do not use a fan or turn lights on or off; either action could generate a dangerous spark.

For the best finish, spray on a dry day: On humid days, moisture can condense on furniture, causing lacquer to whiten. Vacuum or damp-mop your work area to hold down dust. Use dropcloths to protect surfaces from drifting spray.

Lacquer cannot be applied over varnish, paint or most stains; it will dissolve them. Its solvents also cause pigments in such woods as mahogany and rosewood to bleed. To avoid these problems, remove the old finish *(pages 34-35)*, spray on two coats of sanding sealer — a lacquer that seals wood — and sand the surface before applying the finish. To apply clear lacquer over a stain, seal the wood and use a non-grain-raising stain *(page 30)*. Wait 48 hours, then spray with lacquer.

One can of sealer and two of pigmented lacquer covered this table. To coat larger areas, you can buy spraying lacquer in quantity for use in a spray gun *(pages 50-51)*. Brushing lacquer is also available, but it is difficult to apply without leaving brush marks. Lacquer is sold in paint and hardware stores; auto supply dealers also carry aerosol cans of colored lacquer suitable for furniture.

Aerosol cans are easy to use, but keep two things in mind. Heat increases the pressure in the can, so for a strong spray use lacquer at 70° F. or above. However at 120° F. there is danger of explosion; be sure, therefore, to store the can in a cool, dark place.

Spray on at least five coats of lacquer with smooth strokes. Shake the can often to keep the lacquer and propellant mixed *(below)*. You need not sand between coats: Lacquer solvents soften the previous coat enough to ensure bonding. However, light sanding with super-fine (400-grit) sandpaper erases flaws *(Step 4)*.

When the can is empty, spray until all of the gas is released. Then dispose of the can, but do not puncture or incinerate it.

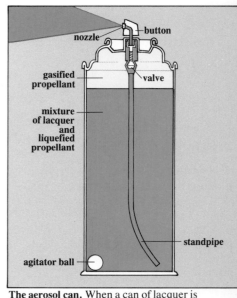

The aerosol can. When a can of lacquer is shaken, an agitator ball mixes the lacquer with a liquefied gas propellant. Pressing the button atop the can opens a valve; the propellant expands and forces the mixture up the standpipe and out the nozzle. The propellant disperses while the lacquer coats the surface with a wet film. Before storing a partly empty can, invert it and press the button briefly. The escaping gas will clear away lacquer that otherwise would dry and clog the nozzle.

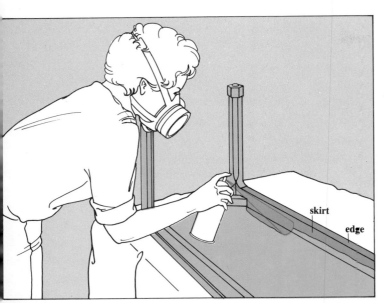

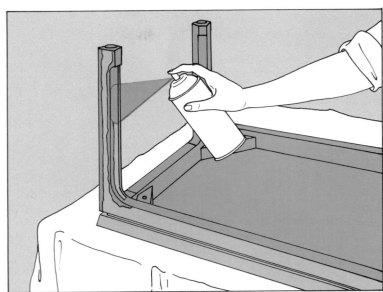

1 **Lacquering the underside.** Rest the table upside down on a protected work surface. Shake the aerosol can vigorously for two minutes. Then aim the nozzle at one end of the table skirt's edge, holding the can 10 to 12 inches from the edge and parallel to it. Press the button firmly and sweep along the edge and back again, keeping equal distance between the can and the surface; release the button at the end of each stroke. Then hold the can at about a 30° angle to the vertical and spray inside the skirt *(above):* Sweep once along the upper part, lower for the next stroke. Make each fresh band of lacquer overlap half of the one before it. Spray the inside of the skirt and all its edges. Then, holding the can parallel to the surface, spray the underside of the table.

2 **Spraying the table's legs.** Hold the aerosol can 10 to 12 inches from one corner of a table leg, and at about a 30° angle to the vertical. Use a single vertical painting stroke to spray a band of lacquer on the corner. Spray a band of lacquer on the remaining corners of the table leg, then spray a band down each face of the leg *(above),* overlapping the strokes sprayed on the corners. Repeat the action for all of the table's legs. Next, holding the can parallel to the surface, use horizontal strokes to spray the outside of the table's skirt, overlapping these strokes as you did on the skirt's inner surface *(Step 1).* Let the piece dry for 20 minutes.

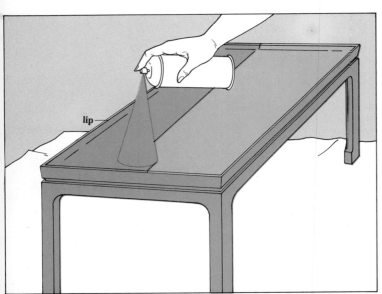

3 **Lacquering the tabletop.** Set the table upright on a dropcloth that covers the floor. Hold the aerosol can 10 to 12 inches from the surface of the tabletop and parallel to the top. Spray the top with lengthwise, overlapping strokes. If the tabletop has a surrounding lip like the one shown here, angle the can upward slightly when applying lacquer to the lip so that you are sure to completely cover the curving area. Let the lacquered piece dry for 20 minutes.

4 **Sanding between coats.** Fit a piece of super-fine (400-grit) sandpaper onto a cushioned sanding block. Lightly sand the level surfaces of the table, working along the grain. Wrap a small piece of sandpaper around your finger to smooth any curves and less accessible areas. Wipe the surface clean of sanding dust with a tack rag *(page 47).* Apply the next coat of lacquer while the table is upright, spraying first the legs, then the sides and top. (The underside does not need additional coats.) Wait 20 minutes, then sand again. Apply a third coat of lacquer, wait 20 minutes, then rub the surface with 4/0 steel wool and wipe it with a tack rag. Rub again with steel wool and clean with the tack rag after the fourth and fifth coats. Then apply paste wax and polish the whole table.

49

Choosing and using an electric sprayer

Long a mainstay of professionals, the electric spray gun has been redesigned for amateurs. Today it offers an economical alternative to aerosol cans, which cost twice as much as bulk paint. A spray gun is indispensable for painting wicker furniture *(pages 52-53)*, whose intricate weave defies brushes. It also is the ideal tool for fine finishes — such as lacquer — that require many thin, perfect coats.

The best sprayer for home use is the airless type, sold at hardware and paint stores, and available from tool-rental shops. Rather than internally mixing paint with compressed gas, as aerosol cans do, this compact sprayer dispenses a jet of pure paint that only atomizes as it emerges from the nozzle. Sprayers with a piston pump *(right)* are the tool of choice for furniture. Avoid airless spray guns that employ a rotating disk: They cannot be sharply angled up or down and have an awkward fan-shaped spray pattern.

Learning to use a spray gun is a trial-and-error business of spraying test bands, adjusting the sprayer or thinning the paint, then testing again *(opposite)*. If the spray still spits and spatters, the viscosity of your finish may require a smaller or larger nozzle from the sprayer's kit. Or the nozzle and atomizer valve may need replacing because their orifices have been enlarged with heavy use.

Though an airless spray gun wastes less paint or enamel in misty overspray than do aerosol cans, it requires equally stringent precautions: Work outdoors or in a garage, cover all nearby surfaces with newspapers or dropcloths, and wear a respirator to guard against paint fumes.

Airless sprayers also require a few special safeguards. Never bring the nozzle close to your skin or to someone else — its high-pressure jet can inject paint through the skin. Do not run the sprayer when it is clogged or its reservoir is dry. If your enamel contains 20 per cent or more of acrylic resins, add a lubricant recommended by the sprayer's manufacturer.

Always clean the sprayer immediately after use: First spray the correct thinner for your paint, then disassemble the sprayer and soak its removable parts in thinner. Before storing the machine, guard against rust by removing the suction tube, squirting a few drops of light oil through its socket into the paint chamber and triggering the sprayer briefly.

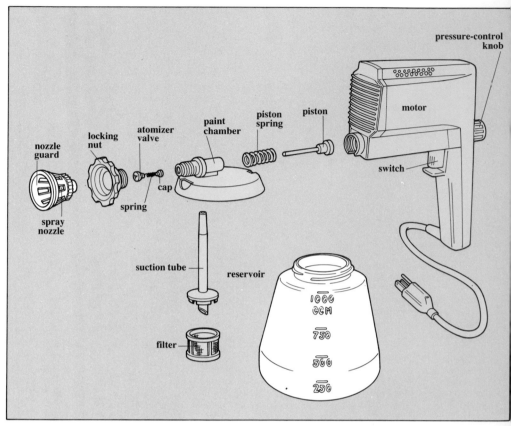

An airless piston sprayer. A sprayer's working parts are concealed within its top, which screws onto a plastic paint reservoir. A motor within the top's housing drives a piston forward about 120 times per second. With each forward stroke the piston seals off a suction tube at the bottom of the paint chamber and drives a spurt of paint or enamel forward through holes in an atomizer valve. As the turbulent, high-pressure stream emerges from the tiny nozzle orifice, the paint disperses into a conical spray pattern.

When the piston's forward stroke ends, a spring-loaded cap seals the paint chamber's outlet while a strong spring drives the piston backward, uncovering the suction tube. The vacuum created by the piston's return stroke then sucks another pulse of paint up the tube into the chamber. A control knob adjusts the length of the piston's stroke, determining the amount of paint pulled into the chamber and hence the eventual spray pattern — the size and diffusion of the droplets.

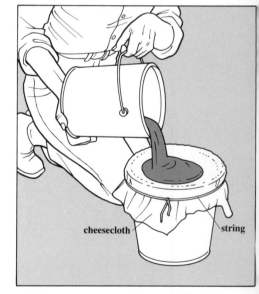

1 **Straining the paint.** Wrap a double layer of cheesecloth loosely over the mouth of a clean 1-gallon paint bucket. Tie the cloth to the bucket's top. Slowly pour enough paint for your furniture — about 2 quarts for a wicker sofa such as the one shown on page 52 — through the cheesecloth into the bucket; untie and discard the cloth. Using a measuring cup, pour 8 fluid ounces of enamel into the reservoir of the sprayer. Then screw on the sprayer's top.

2 **Learning to use the gun.** Set a large card-board box in an area protected by a drop-cloth or newspapers. Plug in the sprayer and turn the pressure-control knob to a medium setting. With its nozzle about 12 inches from the box and perpendicular to the side, sweep the sprayer back and forth across the box with a smooth, flowing motion. For each stroke, squeeze the trigger an instant before the nozzle points at one edge of the box and release it an instant after the spray crosses the opposite edge. Spray a section in several strokes, lapping each band of paint over the lower third of its predecessor. When you are familiar with the technique, spray a single test band in an unpainted area of the box.

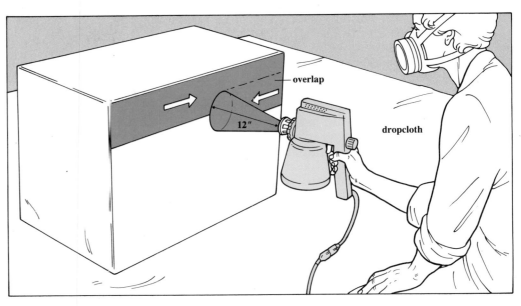

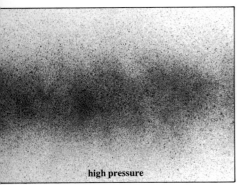
high pressure

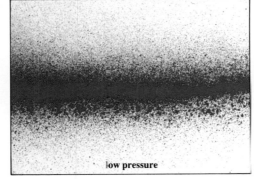
low pressure

correct pressure

3 **Adjusting the pressure.** Study the test band. A band of pinpoint dots of paint reflects high pressure *(above)*. A narrow, heavy band with spattered clumps of paint at its center indicates low pressure *(above, center)*. The correct pressure yields a band about 6 inches high, with a slightly heavier layer of paint at the band's center *(above, right)*. Spray additional test bands as necessary, adjusting the pressure knob to find the optimum setting. If the test band is too heavy even at the highest pressure setting, thin the paint *(Step 4)*.

4 **Thinning the paint.** If pressure adjustments *(Step 3)* do not produce a satisfactory test band, unplug the sprayer and unscrew the reservoir. Use a measuring spoon to pour 2 tablespoons (1 fluid ounce) of thinner into the sprayer's reservoir. Stir the mixture with a paint stick and reassemble the sprayer. Return the pressure knob to a medium setting and spray another test band *(Step 2)*; adjust the pressure accordingly. If the band is still too heavy, add more thinner — 1 tablespoon at a time — until you achieve a good spray pattern. Note the amount of thinner added and use the same dilution for later batches.

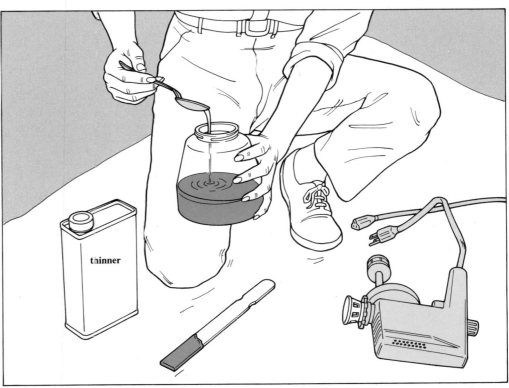

Brightening wicker furniture

Newly enameled wicker furniture such as the settee below gives a bright, summery air to any room. With a spray gun *(pages 50-51)* you can give wicker's durable weave a thin, even coat of enamel, to revitalize an old color or create a new one.

Before readying wicker for finishing, scrape away paint from an inconspicuous strand and examine its fibers. Straight-grained fibers denote pieces made of reed, rattan or willow; twisted fibers indicate wicker made of sea grass or paper.

Chemical stripping of wicker can weaken the furniture's structure and damage the weave. If paint has chipped badly or clogged the weave, wicker with straight-grained fibers can be stripped by a profes-

sional. Wicker composed of twisted fibers should never be stripped.

Already-painted wicker should be cleaned *(Step 1)* before primer or enamel is applied. Straight-grained wicker may be rinsed with a garden hose, but use a minimum of water on twisted fibers lest they unravel. After cleaning, sand the sharp edges around chips in the old finish.

If chipping paint has exposed fibers, prime those spots with a small brush and enamel undercoat in a color close to that of the finish enamel. Tint the undercoat by mixing 10 parts of it with 1 part of the enamel (where the manufacturer's instructions permit this), or with universal colors — concentrated colors in tubes, available in paint stores. When finish-

ing wicker in a new color, or enameling stripped wicker, spray the entire piece with one coat of enamel undercoat.

For already-painted wicker, use high gloss alkyd enamel; one coat is usually sufficient. Stripped wicker can be enameled also or finished with three coats of varnish *(pages 38-39)*, preceded if you like by a stain *(pages 30-31)*.

The intricate weave of wicker demands a special spraying technique. As always, wear a respirator when working, but instead of holding the gun perpendicular to the surface, keep it at a 45° angle and sweep back and forth so the finish penetrates and fully covers the weave. Let the finish dry at least 24 hours before applying a second coat or using the furniture.

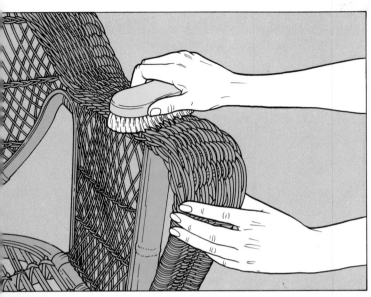

1 **Cleaning wicker furniture.** Clean straight-grained wicker furniture by dipping a soft scrub brush into warm soapy water and washing the entire piece, using a toothbrush to reach inaccessible areas. Then hose off the piece, or rinse it with a wet towel, and wipe it dry. To clean wicker made of twisted fibers, wet a towel with warm soapy water, wring it out and scrub the piece thoroughly. Then rinse it with a clean, damp towel and immediately wipe it dry.

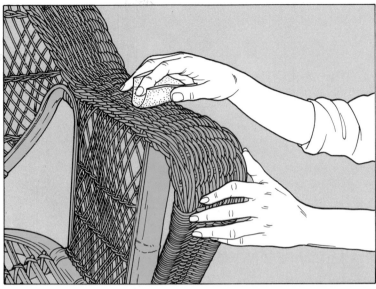

2 **Sanding a chip.** Closely inspect the wicker's surface for chips in the old enamel. Sand the sharp edges around any chips with fine (150-grit) sandpaper *(above)*. Then rub the entire piece with medium (1/0) steel wool to raise a tooth in the old finish; vacuum away dust and loose flakes of enamel. Clean the piece again with a damp cloth, and wipe it dry. Let the piece dry overnight before spraying on the first coat of enamel.

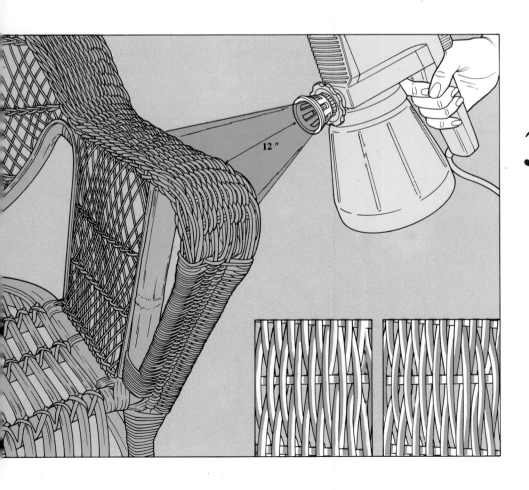

3 **Enameling wicker.** Spray the piece by sections: First invert it and spray the underside; then set the piece upright and spray the back, sides, seat and skirt. For each section, hold the spray gun 12 inches from the wicker surface and tilt the gun at about a 45° angle so the spray hits the fibers from the top and side, allowing the paint to penetrate the weave most completely. Apply a thin coat of enamel, sweeping the gun either horizontally or vertically *(page 51, Step 2)*. Then aim the nozzle at a 45° angle to the unpainted side of the weave and spray the section again. The left-hand inset shows wicker sprayed from the left, and the right-hand inset shows it sprayed from the right. In small areas where it is difficult to maneuver, hold the nozzle at a sharper angle or point it directly at the surface.

The delights of age-old arts

The prancing unicorns and fanciful flowers that decorate the heirloom chests below and at right are 18th Century American versions of a tradition that goes back to the Middle Ages. Originally created by and for peasants, painted furniture often imitated the carving and graining of fine cabinetry or the opulent veining of marble. Painted designs have never gone out of style, and the modern decorator can create heirlooms for tomorrow from a wide variety of techniques: Stenciling makes it possible to repeat motifs with exactitude *(pages 56-63),* and vinegar painting encourages free-style designing *(pages 64-69).* Antiquing mellows new finishes *(pages 70-73).* And marbleizing creates *faux marbre* convincing enough to fool the eye *(pages 74-83),* while bambooing *(pages 84-87)* enhances the joints in real or fake bamboo furniture.

Oddly enough, this custom of gaily painted designs was brought to America primarily by sober, hardworking German farmers. Deeply religious and determinedly pacifist, they were known as Mennonites, Amish, Dunkards and Schwenkfelders. All through the Thirty Years' War, which raged across their homeland from 1618 to 1648, they refused to bear arms, bringing down on themselves the wrath of the authorities. In 1683, when William Penn offered them land and religious freedom in his new colony of Pennsylvania, tens of thousands leaped at the chance. Not all stayed in Pennsylvania. But enough of them did to give their name, Pennsylvania Dutch, (a corruption of *"Deutsch,"* or *"German")* to a unique culture.

Necessarily traveling light, early Pennsylvania Dutch settlers brought from Europe only their most cherished household possessions — stored typically in hinged-top wood chests. Subsequently the chest, or *kiste,* became an important item of furniture in the Pennsylvania Dutch home. Boys as well as girls, upon reaching adolescence, received their own chest for storing personal possessions.

The chests were usually made by the local cabinetmaker, and often it was the cabinetmaker's wife who supplied the decoration. For inspiration, the artists used illustrations in the family Bible, patterns on their woven coverlets, needlework designs, and *fraktur* paintings — the decorative borders of such important family documents as certificates of birth, baptism and marriage.

Among the painters' favorite devices were hearts, birds, stars and tulips, mermaids (associated with childbirth) and Adam and Eve (associated with original sin). After the Revolutionary War, eagles were a popular motif and so were portraits of George and Martha Washington.

Much of the decoration was done freehand, but the artists also took shortcuts. Stencils and wood blocks were used for common design elements, and guidelines for stars, circles and sunbursts were often scribed with compass and ruler.

The paints were bought as powdered pigments and were mixed with such solvents as milk, buttermilk, egg white, homemade varnish, vinegar, even whiskey. No doubt every artist had a favorite formula, to some extent governed by how the paint was to be used. For textured effects it was stroked or daubed on with corks, feathers, sponges and rolled batons of leather. Some textures worked best with one formula, some with another; experience was — as it still is — the only sure way to know which to use.

Compass-drawn stars embellish the lid of this 1791 painted-grain chest.

Three floral panels on Elizabeth Weithknechten's 1805 chest are outlined with ribbed frames that were probably produced by dragging a rolled-up linen or leather baton through the wet paint. The flowers themselves were painted freehand.

Stylized tulips form elaborate candelabra-like patterns on a chest inscribed 1788. A thin wash of green paint forms the background, and the design combines airy freehand tendrils with compass-drawn overlapping circles selectively filled in with paint.

Some of the architectural details on this 1788 chest, made for Margaret Kernen, were created by introducing zigzag patterns into the paint — perhaps with a feather.

Stencils: Simple templates for intricate designs

Stenciling — applying colors through holes in a perforated plate to leave a design on the surface beneath — is thousands of years old. The earliest stencils may have been done by brushing berry juice through a lacy, insect-eaten leaf. Similar techniques and modern materials — artist's acrylic paints and plastic stencil plates — produced the designs on the chest below.

Good stenciling invariably starts with a good background. The surface must be smooth enough for the plate to lie flat and keep paint from seeping under the edges of its holes. At the same time, the surface cannot be glossy: Stencil paints will not adhere to an untextured finish. The acrylic stencil paints used here need a flat latex background, which has a microscopic roughness for them to bond to. When the stenciling is completed, the entire piece of furniture should be covered with clear polyurethane varnish *(pages 44-45)* to protect the pattern and the latex paint.

Readily available at hobby and art-supply stores, the materials required for stenciling are simple: paints, a stencil brush for each color, and stencil plates. Artist's acrylic paints are quick-drying and clean up with soapy water. They come in tubes or jars, and in dozens of colors, which you can mix easily. Stencil brushes are available in many sizes; choose those proportional to your design. Durable stencil plates are made from transparent sheet plastic, 7 mils thick and frosted on one side so you can draw on them with a pencil. Precut plates are available, but the techniques in Steps 2-6 will enable you to make your own. Cut them on a smooth board, using a craft knife with a sharp No. 11 (pointed) blade.

A one-color design requires only one plate, of course, but you can apply more than one color with a single plate if the areas of different colors are separated by at least ½ inch. Otherwise, different colors call for separate plates. Include register marks — partial outlines of the first plate's cutouts — on each subsequent plate, to help you align them when you are painting.

The distinctive look of many stenciled designs derives from their ties — narrow reinforcing strips of plate material left in place across a cutout area *(Step 3)*. Ties leave bands of background color within the painted stencil. The leafy border on this blanket chest has ties; the flower medallion does not.

As you stencil, wash each plate with soapy water after use, and dry it with a towel. This prevents paint build-up in the cutouts and keeps your work looking crisp. Let the acrylic paint dry for at least 24 hours before applying varnish.

Stencil patterns. The floral medallion and the leafy border pattern here are the starting point for the designs on the blanket chest at left. The grid overlying the patterns facilitates enlarging or reducing them (*Step 2*) onto tracing paper; the patterns are then traced onto plastic plates. The medallion requires one plate for each color. The leaves require two plates made as mirror images (*Step 4*) to produce symmetrical borders.

tie

1 **Trying out your design.** Make rough sketches of your design in several sizes, cut them out and try them on the piece of furniture. Tape them in various placements and look at them from a distance. When you have decided on the exact size and place for each decoration, mark the locations precisely by sticking pieces of masking tape on the furniture, positioning the edges of the tape at the edges of the design.

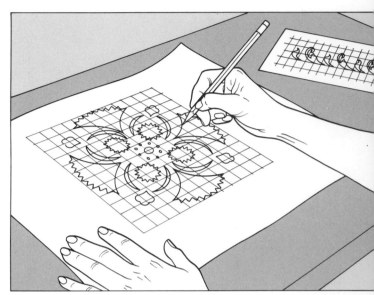

2 **Enlarging or reducing the design.** On tracing paper, plot an area the size you have decided your medallion pattern should be, and rule it off into the same number of squares as in the medallion's grid (page 57). Number and letter your squares correspondingly, then copy the content of each square of the medallion into the matching square on the tracing paper. When you have transferred the contents of every square, go over your outlines with the pencil to give them a smooth, fluid look; then go over them again with a fine-tipped waterproof marker, for clean tracing lines. Apply the same method to the border pattern.

If you are making stencil plates from some other image, start by drawing a grid over your chosen design; then proceed as above.

5 **Cutting the plates.** Tape the first plate to the cutting board, frosted side up. Hold the craft knife in your hand like a pencil and begin cutting along a line, pulling the knife toward you. Turn the cutting board as you cut so that you are always pulling the knife toward you. Cut out all the shapes on the plate. If you make an error in cutting, apply frosted cellophane tape to the front and back of the plate over the mistaken cut, then cut the shape out again. When all the shapes on the first plate are cut out, remove it from the cutting board and cut out the second plate. Repeat these steps to cut the two mirror-image border stencils.

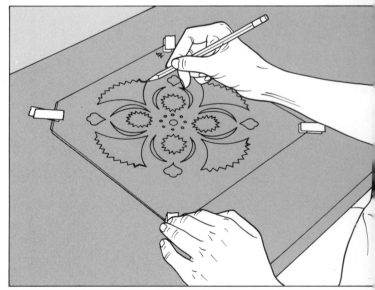

6 **Making register marks.** Tape medallion plate 1 onto your work surface, then tape plate 2 in place over it, with the designs on the two plates perfectly aligned. Use a pencil to trace, on plate 2, parts of three or four of the cutouts of plate 1. Choose areas that are near the edges and widely separated from each other; this will make it easy later to align plate 2 over the image made by stenciling with plate 1.

The border plates do not need register marks; since the leaves at both ends are identical, you can extend the border design by placing the end leaf over the last one stenciled.

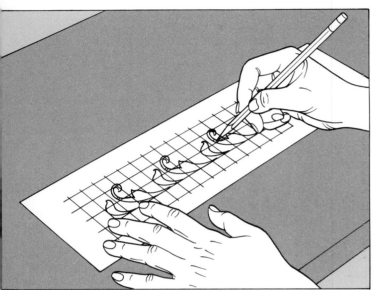

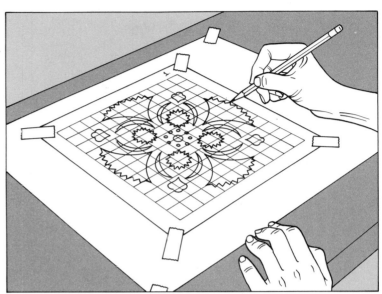

3 **Adding ties and plotting colors.** Where there is a long, narrow cutout in the design *(above)* or where a cutout area encircles a solid area, add reinforcing ties across the cutout area — each consisting of two parallel lines at least 1/16 inch apart. Color in the design with colored pencils, to create a master design for reference while stenciling. If the design requires more than one stencil plate, decide which parts of the design will appear on each plate, and mark them accordingly on the design. Mark equal borders of at least ½ inch on all sides of the design, and use this outline as a template to cut a piece of frosted sheet plastic for each plate.

4 **Tracing the plates.** Tape the master design to the work surface, then tape the plastic for the first plate over it, frosted side up. With a sharp pencil, write the numeral 1 on one corner of the plate, then trace all the parts of the design that belong on this plate. Tape the second plate over the first, aligning the edges exactly. Number the second plate with the numeral 2 and trace the parts of the design that belong on it. Cut about an inch off the top left corner of each plate so that later you can tell at a glance whether the plates are oriented correctly. To make mirror-image border stencils, first trace the border design onto the first border plate; then turn the tracing paper over and trace the reversed design onto the second plate. Number and notch these plates.

7 **Getting ready to paint.** Align plate 1 with the masking-tape markers on the furniture *(above, left)*, then secure the plate with masking tape. Do the same with the first border stencil, taking care to keep it parallel with the edge of the furniture *(above, right)*; remove the markers for both plates. Make a palette of several thicknesses of newspaper, then measure out on the palette ½ tablespoon of each color you will use with these plates. Set out a separate brush for each color. Dip a brush into the first color, then work off the excess paint onto the palette with a few up-and-down "pouncing" movements. When the brush leaves a mark that is moist but not soupy, you are ready to paint. ▶

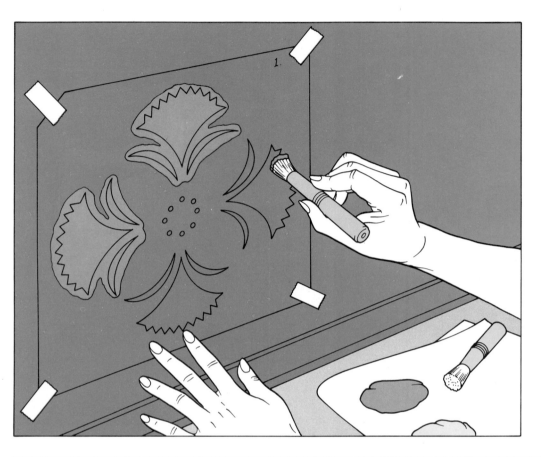

8 **Applying paint.** Brush the paint on, working from the edges of each cutout area toward its center, using very short, light strokes and keeping the brush perpendicular to the surface. Each time the brush gets dry, load it again with paint, and pounce out the excess. If the brush begins to stiffen with dried paint, wash it in soapy water, rinse and dry it well, then load it again with paint. As soon as all of the cutouts are filled, lift the plate off the surface — taking care not to smear the paint. Wash and dry the plate before reusing it. Apply paint through the first border plate similarly.

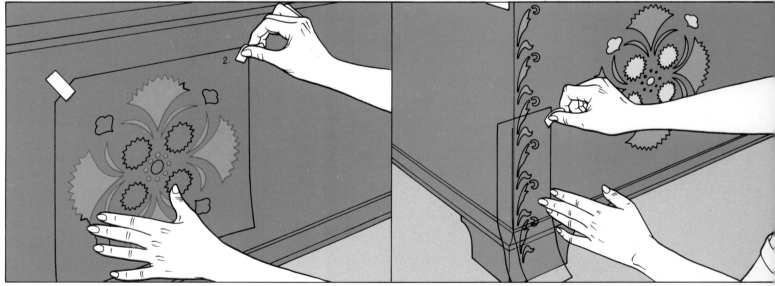

9 **Lining up the second plate.** Allow the paint applied through the first medallion plate to dry for at least 10 minutes, then position plate 2 by lining up its register marks over the painted areas (*above, left*). Tape the plate to the surface and apply paints as you did through plate 1. To continue stenciling the border pattern, align the cutout area at one end of the first border plate over the last painted area (*above, right*). Tape the plate in place, taking care to keep it parallel to the edge of the furniture, and apply paint through the plate as before.

Achieving subtle shades with japan paints

The delicacy of the morning glories on the rocking chair at left contrasts vividly with the boldness of the motifs that decorate the chest on page 56, yet all of the designs were applied through the same kind of stencil plates. The subtle gradations of color in the morning glories are achieved by applying premixed japan paints — highly pigmented, fast-drying, oil-based paints — with a barely moist stencil brush. Although the brush deposits only a faint smudge of paint with each stroke, repetition builds up more paint particles, creating darker and darker shades.

The stencil plates are traced and cut like those used with artist's acrylic paints (*pages 58-59*). However, you are more likely to need a separate plate for each color, or each shade, in your design because the circular brushstrokes leave paint on the plate for ½ inch or more around each opening. One plate can be used for two colors — or two shades of the same color — only if the cutouts for different colors are at least an inch apart.

Japan paints are available from hobby or paint stores, in dozens of mixable colors. They adhere to any kind of paint or enamel, provided it is not glossy. Since the paints dry quickly on the palette, set out only a little of one color at a time.

Before you stencil the furniture, test the colors and practice the technique on a board painted the color of the piece of furniture. Watch the build-up of paint so you can tell when you have achieved the desired shade. Keep in mind that many japan paints look darker when they dry.

You can use each plate several times before cleaning it. When paint begins to build up in the corners of the openings, lay the plate on several layers of clean paper towels and wipe it with a rag dipped in mineral spirits. Let the plate dry completely before you use it again. If a brush begins to stiffen with dried paint as you work, wipe it with a rag dipped in mineral spirits and dry it on clean paper towels.

After the stencil paint has had three days to harden, cover the entire piece of furniture with a coat of alkyd varnish (*pages 44-45*). Test the varnish first over the paints on your practice board; if any of the colors run, apply a sealer coat of 5-pound-cut shellac that has been diluted with an equal part of denatured alcohol.

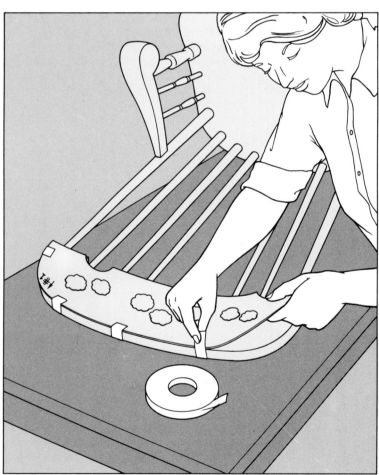

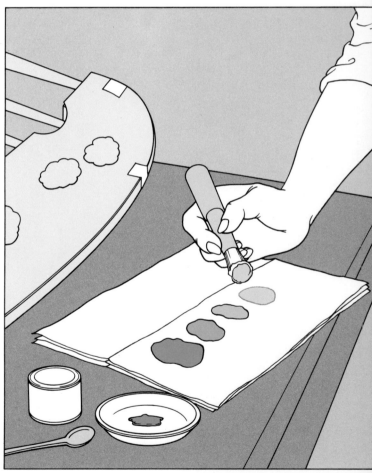

1 **Positioning the first plate.** Place the furniture at a comfortable working height and secure it against wobbling. Using short strips of masking tape, firmly attach the first stencil plate to the furniture. Then find a working position for yourself that will allow you to look at the design right side up as you work; even if your position is awkward, you need a head-on view in order to achieve a natural-looking result.

2 **Getting ready to paint.** Using a disposable spoon, put a teaspoon of the first color of japan paint onto a plastic-coated paper plate and recap the paint can. Dip a clean, dry stencil brush lightly into the paint so that paint covers ⅛ inch of the bristles. Press the brush lightly and repeatedly against a palette made of four or more layers of paper towels, until the paint is distributed evenly at the tips of the bristles. Then, holding the brush vertical, move it in circles against the palette, lifting it and moving to a new area every few seconds. The brush will leave lighter and lighter deposits of paint; when three or four circular strokes leave an airy, almost dry spot of color, the brush is ready to use.

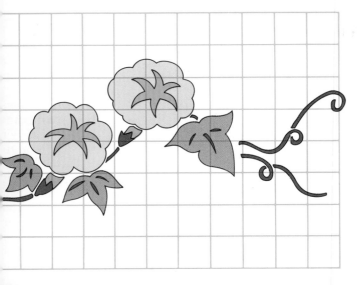

Making the stencil plates. Follow the directions on page 58, Step 2, to enlarge or reduce the pattern at left. Plan to produce a separate plate for each color or shade of the pattern — in this case, four plates are used. If, as here, the stencil will fit onto a small section of a piece of furniture, cut the plates to the shape of that section for easy handling. Then transfer the stencil pattern and cut out the plates (*pages 58-59, Steps 3-6*).

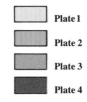

Plate 1

Plate 2

Plate 3

Plate 4

Applying the first color. Stand the brush at the edge of one opening in the stencil plate, and begin making clockwise circles that extend halfway over the plate and halfway over the opening. Simultaneously move the brush around the edge of the opening. Go completely around without lifting the brush, then go around in the other direction, making counterclockwise circles with the brush. Apply paint through the rest of the openings on the stencil plate in the same way, loading the brush as shown in Step 2 before starting on each opening. The paint dries very quickly; you can remove the stencil plate immediately.

Adding dark accents. Tape the second stencil plate in position, then load the brush as shown in Step 2, using the same color you used for the first plate. Apply paint through one opening, working with a back-and-forth sweeping motion from the outside of the opening toward the center. Fill the opening evenly, continuing to add paint as necessary to make these stenciled areas darker than those you painted in Step 3. Fill in the remaining openings in the same way, and untape the plate.

If your design includes another set of colors, as in this case, repeat Steps 1 through 4 to complete the design.

Bold patterns with vinegar paint

Humble furniture such as the cabinet below can be transformed into a boldly patterned work of art by the early-19th Century American craft of vinegar painting. The two-toned effect that characterizes this imaginative finish is produced by applying vinegar paint — a mixture of ordinary vinegar and powdered pigments — over semigloss enamel. Then, while the paint is still wet, such varied implements as sponges, corks, corncobs and feathers are pressed into the paint to form designs silhouetted against the enamel beneath.

Although any color combination is possible, dull orange enamel topped by a vinegar paint tinted with burnt umber is traditional; the effect is shown here. Other common pairings are dull yellow enamel and vinegar paint tinted with either burnt umber or raw sienna *(pages 66-69)*.

The preliminary for vinegar painting is developing a plan. Once the paint is applied, it will dry within 10 minutes, so you must know in advance what designs you want to make and have the gear assembled for creating them. Techniques for duplicating the designs on this cabinet are demonstrated on the next two pages; other designs are shown on pages 66-69.

Whatever designs you select, use them symmetrically. Keep the pattern on both ends of a chest or cabinet the same, for example, and center large designs such as sunbursts on a door panel or tabletop.

When you are ready to start, enamel the piece of furniture *(pages 46-47),* plus a scrap of wood to practice on. After the last coat of enamel dries, mix the vinegar paint. A cupful will cover about 20 square feet, with enough left over for practicing. For the paint, you will need the kind of

powdered pigment that paint stores se for tinting mortar and grout. Measure ¼ cup of pigment into a glass bowl. Stir in ¼ cup of cider vinegar or distilled white vin egar to form a smooth paste. Slowly mi in ¾ cup of additional vinegar.

Brush on the paint one small section a a time. If the paint strokes will show through the design, apply them neatly i parallel lines; otherwise, scrub on th paint casually with a circular motion. A you work, stir the paint to keep it mixed If you do not like a pattern, wipe it awa with a rag moistened in vinegar or water

Let the finished vinegar paintings dr overnight. To protect them, apply a thi coat of clear semigloss alkyd varnish di luted with an equal amount of turpentine followed by two coats of full-strength var nish. Sand lightly between coats wit super-fine (400-grit) sandpaper.

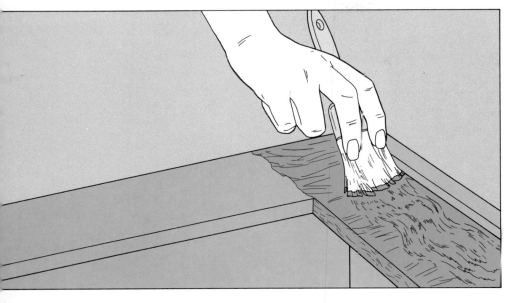

1 **Making waves.** Dip the tip of a 1½-inch nylon-bristle brush into vinegar paint and brush a thin layer onto a small area of a piece of enameled furniture — here, the frame of a cabinet. Then, grasp a dry brush of the same size and type just below the ferrule, and pinch the bristles apart with your thumb and first two fingers. Lay the bristle tips in the still-wet paint, and stroke lengthwise while wriggling the brush from side to side to make a wavy pattern. Periodically, lift the brush and change the direction of the stroke, being sure to overlap already-painted areas. As you work, wipe the bristles of the brush with a cloth or paper towel to remove excess paint.

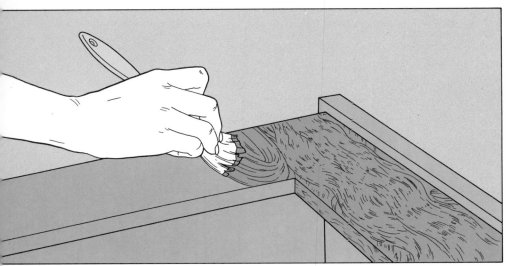

2 **Wetting a dry edge.** To start each new area, brush a thin layer of paint over the dry edge of the first coat on the adjacent completed area. Then brush a thin layer of the paint onto the rest of the new area and, with a dry brush, continue making the pattern. If at any time the paint dries before you finish an area, brush a fresh coat over the dry edge before proceeding.

3 **Creating a mottled texture.** Cut an egg-sized piece from a natural sponge. Brush vinegar paint onto a small area of the furniture piece — here, a door panel. Then dab the sponge all over the paint. If, as you proceed, the pattern texture becomes less distinct, blot the sponge on a cloth to remove excess paint. ▶

4 **Forming fan shapes.** Stand a stiff cardboard rectangle — here, 2 inches by 4 inches — on edge in wet vinegar paint with one corner of the cardboard lodged in a corner of the door panel. Drag the cardboard about ¼ inch by its outer end. Lift the cardboard and swing it ¼ inch, then repeat the dragging, lifting and swinging to create a quarter-circle fan in each corner and a full circle in the center.

5 **Forming bars.** Cut a rectangular piece of synthetic sponge about 2 by 1 by ½ inch. Brush vinegar paint onto the frame and edges of the door. Press the narrow edge of the sponge onto the frame to form a continuous border of stripes at right angles to the door's outer edges. Then use a natural sponge *(Step 3)* to give a mottled look to the door's edges.

A Spider-Web Design

1 **Making a sunburst.** Brush vinegar paint onto an enameled surface. Grasp a small dried corncob by its ends, and press it lightly into the wet surface at irregular intervals to create an overall texture. Then, holding one end in place, drag and lift the cob *(Step 4, above)* to form a sunburst in the center and fans at the corners.

2 **Outlining with a cork.** Press a bottle cork into the still-wet paint around the outside edge of the corncob sunburst pattern *(left)*. Lift the cork and press it down at the edge of the first impression. Repeat until the sunburst is encircled *(photograph, right)*. To alter the pattern, cut holes or jagged lines into the cork with a sharp knife.

Sinuous Streaks of Color

Making irregular striations. Brush a thin coat of vinegar paint onto an enameled surface. Hold an artist's feather by its quill and run your fingers down the sides of the feather to separate the vanes and roughen their edges. Then draw the feather through the wet paint — wavering it slightly as you go. Its ruffled edges will create irregular streaks or stripes like those in the photograph at right. After each stroke, wipe the excess vinegar paint off the feather with a cloth.

A Wild-Flower Motif

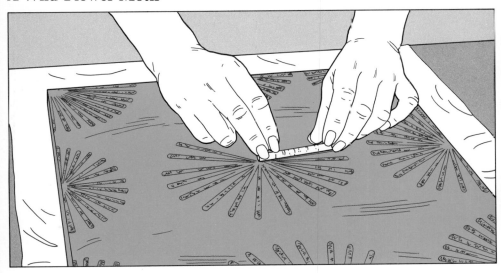

Making flower petals. Cut a 3-inch-square section of newspaper. Roll it in the shape of a slim cigarette and tape the edge closed. Working in the direction of the grain, brush a thin coat of vinegar paint onto an enameled surface. Hold one end of the newspaper roll stationary, then press the roll into the wet paint. Lift the free end of the roll, move it about ¼ inch and press it once more into the paint. Repeat this action to make the petals of the flower pattern shown in the photograph at right.

A Pattern of Pickets and Cobblestones

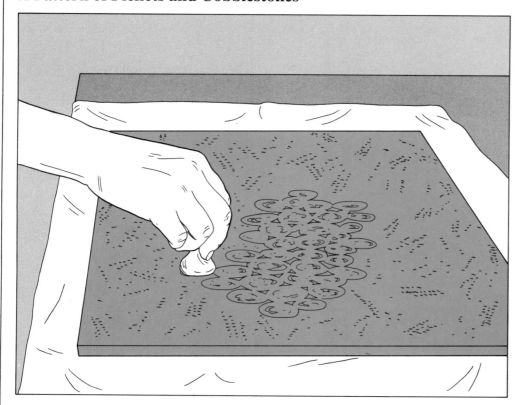

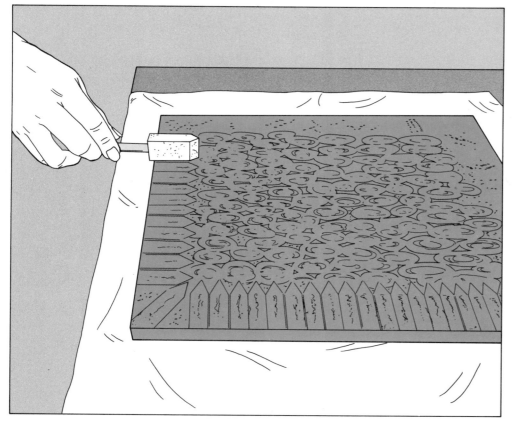

1 **Simulating cobblestones.** Roll a walnut-sized piece of modeling clay into a ball, or use glazing compound sold at hardware stores for installing glass. Apply a thin coat of vinegar paint onto an enameled surface. Dab the paint with a corncob to texture it (*page 66, lower left*). Then repeatedly press the ball into the wet paint to form a cluster of adjoining circles resembling cobblestones. Blot the ball on a cloth when paint accumulates on it.

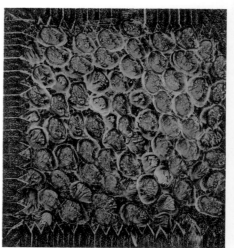

2 **Creating a picket border.** While the paint is still wet, press the side of a foam-tipped paint applicator into it repeatedly to form a continuous border around the enameled surface. Periodically blot the applicator on a cloth to remove vinegar paint absorbed by the foam.

Two Basket-Weave Effects

1 Forming basket weave. Brush vinegar paint onto enamel. Grasp a dry 1½-inch brush by the ferrule and press the bristles into the paint; then lift the brush — without dragging the bristles. Make an identical brush mark beside the first, then turn the brush and form two similar rectangles at right angles to the first pair.

2 Making ringlets. Holding the 1½-inch natural-bristle brush by its ferrule, place the bristle tips on the wet paint. Move the brush in an arc. Lift the brush, clean the bristles and set them where the first stroke ended. Repeat the arcing motion until the pattern row is complete. Begin the next row slightly overlapping the first.

A Tortoise-Shell Look

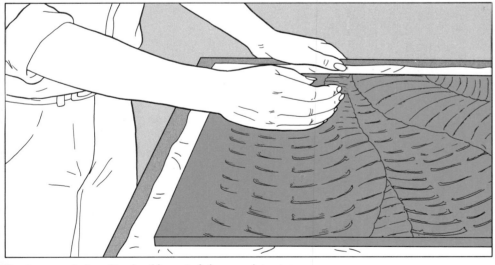

Shaping curve designs. Brush a thin coat of vinegar paint onto an enameled surface. Place the side of your hand on the surface in a relaxed curved position. Sweep your hand crosswise in a gentle arc, while lightly bouncing your hand up and down. From time to time, change the direction in which you are sweeping your hand, being sure to overlap old curves with new ones. Periodically clean your hand with a cloth.

Emulating the patina of time

One of the most appealing characteristics of a fine old piece of painted furniture is its mellow, timeworn appearance. This rich patina is difficult to reproduce, but it can be approximated by a simple process known as antiquing.

Antiquing is not a finish for valuable antiques, or for furniture with a beautiful wood grain that deserves to be emphasized by a clear finish. It is best used on unfinished furniture, or to enliven pieces of uninteresting design. You may wish to distress the piece (pages 32-33) before painting to encourage an aged look.

In antiquing, a dark, translucent glaze (opposite, Steps 2-4) is applied over a dry base coat of paint or enamel. While the glaze is still wet, it is partially removed to leave a subtle, uneven finish, which softens the base color and emphasizes the lines of the piece of furniture, as the antiqued table seen here demonstrates.

Three different tactics (page 72) can be used to remove and manipulate the glaze. Striating, or striping, creates a pattern similar to that of wood grain and enhances furniture of rustic or simple lines, such as this table. Stippling creates spots or blotches, which can become a subtle finish for more delicate pieces of furniture. The third method, wiping, mimics the effect of years of natural wear by removing glaze in areas, such as chair arms, that would receive the most use, while leaving an accumulation of glaze in carved recesses. Pieces that have been striated or stippled can also be made to imitate the effects of wear; after the glaze dries, rub the areas that should show heavy use with fine steel wool.

The most satisfactory base coat for the glaze is a semigloss or flat paint, which is allowed to dry and then followed by a coat of diluted shellac (Step 1, opposite). The shellac provides a smooth surface that allows the glaze to flow on easily, and it also serves as a protective barrier between the paint and glaze. A cloth dampened in mineral spirits — a paint thinner to which shellac is impervious — removes glaze from the surface without damaging the base coat.

When painting the piece, also coat a scrap of wood for use as a test board. Brushing the glaze onto the board will show how the glaze will appear on the piece of furniture, and provide an opportunity to experiment with different antiquing effects.

A clear antiquing glaze can be purchased in paint or hardware stores, but you can economically mix one of your own. The glaze is tinted to a darker tone than the base paint with artist's oil paint. Earth tones, such as raw umber, make appealing glazes that are compatible with most paint colors. But you can also experiment with other colors, such as deeper shades of the base paint (page 72).

When you determine the color, mix enough glaze to do the entire piece; a cupful will cover a large piece — even a dining-room table — and provide enough excess to allow for practice. Brush the glaze onto one section of the piece at a time, in an area no larger than 2 feet by 3 feet. Let the glaze become slightly tacky — allow about three to five minutes — before starting to work with it. If the glaze dries before you are done, dampen a rag with mineral spirits and wipe off the glaze entirely. Then begin afresh with more glaze.

After you are done, allow the antiqued finish to cure for at least 48 hours. Then apply a protective coating of clear varnish (pages 44-45).

Preparing the Surface and the Glaze

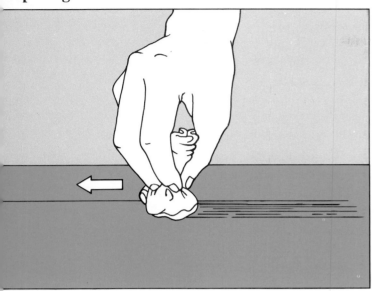

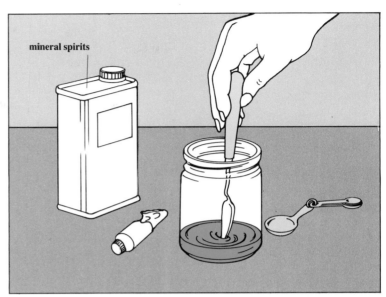

mineral spirits

1 **Coating the paint with shellac.** Pour ½ cup of 5-pound-cut shellac *(page 42)* into a glass bowl. Dilute the shellac with ½ cup of denatured alcohol and stir the mixture. Use a natural-bristle brush or a disposable applicator made from a knee-high nylon stocking to apply the shellac. To make the applicator, roll the foot of the stocking into a ball, then twist the open end of the stocking and turn it back over the ball. Twist and turn back the stocking again, then tightly wrap masking tape just above the ball. Grasp the completed applicator by the masking-tape handle, and dip it halfway into the shellac. Working with the grain, use a painting stroke to cover the piece with shellac *(above)*. Let it dry for one hour.

2 **Diluting the oil paint.** Squeeze a 4-inch cylinder (about 4 teaspoons) of artist's oil paint into a small jar. Add 2 tablespoons of mineral spirits to the jar and stir the mixture with a palette knife to form a paste *(above)*. In another jar, combine 2 ounces each of mineral spirits, boiled linseed oil and semigloss varnish; add 1 ounce of japan drier — a product available in paint and hardware stores to accelerate the drying times of oil-based paints and varnishes. Stir the ingredients thoroughly with the palette knife to create 7 ounces, or 14 tablespoons, of clear glaze.

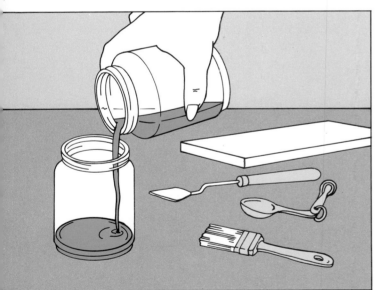

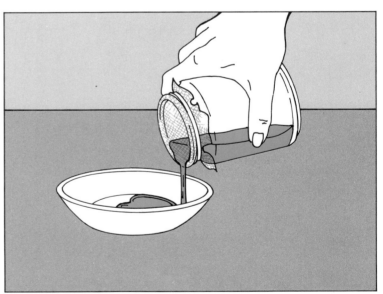

3 **Adjusting the glaze.** Pour about half of the clear glaze into the jar holding the diluted oil paint and stir. Brush a stroke or two of the colored glaze onto a painted-and-shellacked test board. The glaze should have a creamlike consistency. If it is too thick, or if its color is too intense, adjust it by adding clear glaze a tablespoon at a time, testing after each addition. Finish glazing the test board. Note the time required for the glaze to become slightly tacky — usually three to five minutes — then wipe it off with a cloth to see the effect the color of the glaze will have on the base paint. Dampen another cloth with mineral spirits and wipe the glaze completely off the test board; you will need it for the next step.

4 **Straining the colored glaze.** Place a piece of nylon stocking over the jar's mouth, and secure it with a string or rubber band. Pour the glaze through the nylon into a glass bowl to remove any sediment. Then begin the antiquing process, following the instructions for one of the methods described on the next two pages. First practice on the clean test board. Then antique the piece, working on one element at a time.

Three Decorative Effects

Striation
The wood-grain effect above is achieved by dragging the bristles of a dry brush through the glaze, to form parallel bands and lines of color. This piece was painted light green, then striated with a glaze tinted with four hues of artist's oil paints: ½ teaspoon of black, 1 teaspoon each of raw umber and white, and 2 teaspoons of viridian green.

Wiping
The look of age on this carved section is produced by applying glaze to a painted surface and then wiping most of it off, leaving less glaze in areas meant to appear worn and thick deposits in recessed areas. The piece was painted light blue. The glaze was tinted with 1 teaspoon of black and 4 teaspoons of ultramarine artist's oil paint.

Stippling
This soft, mottled appearance is created by stippling — bouncing a glaze-filled brush over a painted surface, then repeating the action with a dry brush. The piece was given a base coat of orange-red paint, then was stippled with a glaze tinted with 4 teaspoons of burnt umber and 2 teaspoons of raw umber artist's oil paint.

Wiping Methods

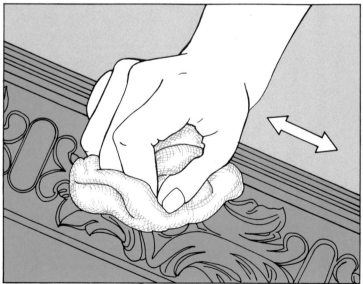

1 **Rubbing off the glaze.** Brush the glaze over a section of the furniture with a 2-inch natural-bristle brush. If the area is carved, as here, work the glaze into all grooves. Let it stand for three to five minutes, then wipe it off with a soft, lint-free cloth, such as cheesecloth. Rub along the grain, wiping harder on high points of carvings *(above)* and in the centers of panels and tabletops to simulate the effect of wear.

2 **Blending with a brush.** Remove some of the excess glaze from the recessed areas by lightly stroking those areas with a dry 1-inch natural-bristle brush *(above)*. Clean the glaze from the brush by wiping the bristles on a rag after every two or three strokes. Soften the gradations from light to dark areas of glaze color on panels or tabletops with light painting strokes of the dry brush; periodically clean the brush.

Striating Methods

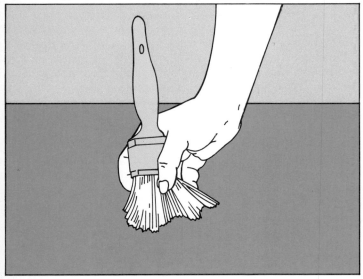

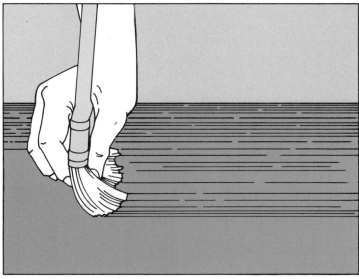

1 **Holding the brush.** Dip a 2-inch natural-bristle brush halfway into the glaze, and tap the bristles lightly against the rim of the bowl. Working along the grain, brush the glaze quickly onto the painted surface. Let it stand for three to five minutes. Then pick up a dry brush of the same size and type as the first one, grasping the bristles just under the ferrule — the metal band around the bristles. Spread the bristles apart in an irregular pattern by pinching them with your fingers (*above*).

2 **Striating the surface.** Begin at the edge of the surface and draw the dry brush through the still-wet glaze, applying enough pressure to bend the bristles. Work in the direction of the grain, using continuous strokes from one end of the surface to the other. To remove glaze picked up by the bristles, wipe the brush on a rag after each stroke.

Stippling Methods

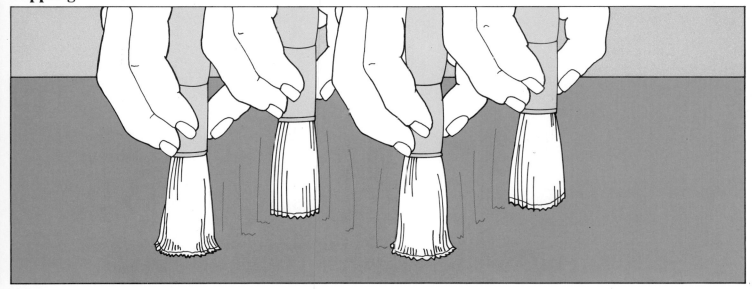

Applying and removing glaze. Dip the tip of a No. 6 oval sash brush or stencil brush into the colored glaze. Remove the excess glaze by tapping the bristles on newspaper until the glaze leaves a soft, mottled pattern. Then hold the brush perpendicular to the furniture surface and lightly bounce it up and down on the base coat of paint. Cover the surface of the furniture with glaze, and let it stand for three to five minutes. Dry the brush by wiping it on a rag, then go over the section with it again, bouncing the dried brush the same way to remove excess glaze; clean the brush often by wiping it on a rag.

Mimicking marble with paint

Marble-topped furniture can command a high price. But a marble imitation realistic enough to fool any but the sharpest eye — the chest top below, for example — can be had for the price of a little paint and patience. To produce such a likeness, you need only artist's oil paints and glaze *(box, opposite)*, brushes, feathers and foam-tipped applicators, and mineral spirits to clean the tools.

Start by removing the top from the furniture; set it on a covered worktable. If you cannot remove the top, cover the area below its edge with masking tape.

Marbleizing begins with the application of semigloss enamel *(pages 46-47),* followed by diluted shellac *(page 71, Step 1).* When you enamel and shellac the furniture's top, also coat a scrap of wood. Practice the marbleizing techniques on it before attempting them on the furniture.

Steps for achieving the black-and-gold chest top below and four other marbleizing projects are described at right and on the following pages. For most of the projects, glaze is applied over the shellac. Only a small amount is needed: Six ounces covers more than 6 square feet.

Marbleizing is done while the glaze is wet, to allow the artist's oil paint to float above the enamel undercoat, giving an illusion of depth. The glaze will stay wet for about 30 minutes, but work on an area only 2 feet square until you are comfortable with the techniques. If the glaze begins to dry, apply more. When you complete a section and glaze the next, reglaze the edge of the finished area so the sections meld into a continuous pattern.

Have a piece of marble — or a picture of real or imitated marble — at hand as you work so you can copy its veins, cloudy-appearing fossil areas and variations in color. No two pieces of marble are identical, so your version need not match perfectly. If you paint a pattern you dislike, wet a cloth with mineral spirits and wipe it away. Then begin afresh with glaze.

Let the marbleized piece dry for 48 hours. Then apply six coats of clear alkyd varnish *(page 45),* sanding lightly after the fourth coat with 400-grit wet-and-dry paper soaked in soapy water. Polish the dry surface with a paste of rottenstone — a fine limestone powder — and mineral oil, followed by a coat of paste wax.

To prepare 6 ounces — ¾ of a measuring cup — of all-purpose glaze, suitable for any marbleizing project, measure the following ingredients into a small jar:

5 tablespoons mineral spirits
3 tablespoons boiled linseed oil
3 tablespoons semigloss clear alkyd varnish
1 tablespoon japan drier

Stir the mixture thoroughly with a palette knife. Put a lid on the jar and keep the glaze tightly covered until you are ready to use it. Then pour as much of the glaze as necessary into a shallow glass bowl.

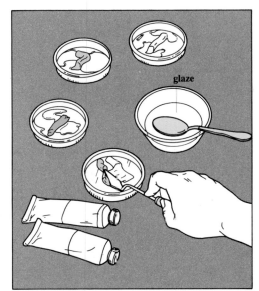

1 **Assembling paints.** Enamel the surface with black semigloss alkyd, shellac it, then prepare glaze. Collect four small, flat dishes or — as here — jar tops. Into one dish, squeeze a ½-inch length (about ½ teaspoon) of white oil paint. Put ½ inch of raw sienna and burnt sienna into separate dishes. Pour 1 teaspoon of glaze around each paint. For the chief veining color, mix ½ inch each of white and raw sienna and 2 teaspoons of glaze with a palette knife.

2 **Glazing the surface.** Dip the wedge-shaped top of a foam-tipped applicator into the bowl of glaze. Using painting strokes that follow the direction of the grain, cover the painted-and-shellacked surface of the furniture top with a thin coat of glaze.

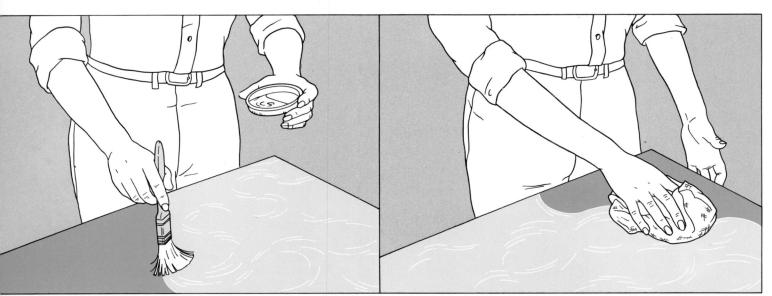

3 **Scrubbing on background color.** While the glaze is still wet, dip the tip of a 1-inch natural-bristle brush into the dish holding white oil paint. Moisten the bristles first with the paint, then with the glaze surrounding it. Apply the paint to the furniture top with a circular scrubbing motion (*above, right*). Move the brush in every direction, covering the surface with paint, but depositing varying amounts of paint in different areas. Then crumple a soft, lint-free cloth — cheesecloth, for example — and lightly dab the furniture top (*above, right*) to remove excess paint and leave a shadowy white color on the background. ▶

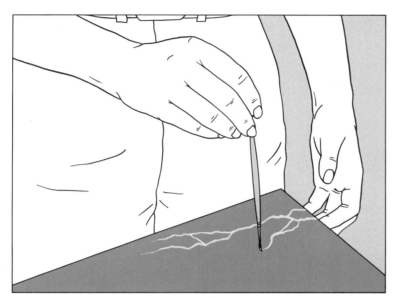

4 **Painting a marble vein.** Hold the top of the handle of a No. 2 artist's brush upright between your thumb and first two fingers; this grip will help you make a fidgety movement with the brush when painting. Dip the tips of the brush's bristles into the chief veining color *(prepared in Step 1)*. Beginning at an edge of the furniture top, lightly draw the bristle tips along the surface to make an irregular, meandering line that mimics one of those in the one-third-scale close-up photograph opposite. Vary the width of this simulated vein occasionally by exerting gentle pressure on the brush. Vary the direction of the vein by turning the brush to the right or left every few inches. Add secondary veins that branch off at shallow angles from the first *(above)*.

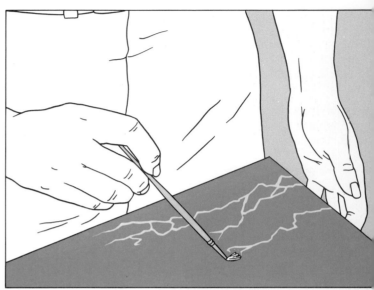

5 **Adding a wide patch of color.** At various intervals while painting the vein, hold the brush at about a 45° angle to the surface and press down on it so that the bristles spread flat. Then twirl the brush with your fingers and thumb so that the bristles roll sideways, leaving a wide, irregularly shaped patch of color. Raise the brush to an upright position and continue with the veining line.

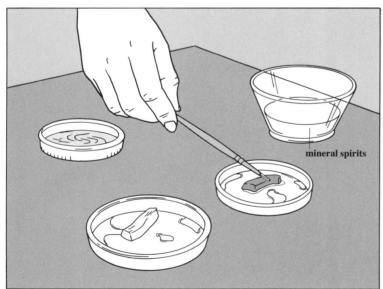

6 **Double-loading the brush.** To vary the colors in the wide patches, you will need to load the bristles with more than one color of paint. Rinse the No. 2 artist's brush in mineral spirits and wipe it dry on a cloth. Draw one side of the bristles against the white paint in the jar top and the other side of the bristles against the burnt sienna or the raw sienna paint *(above)*. Next, dip the bristle tips into the chief veining color. Paint a thin vein, then press down on the brush and roll the bristles sideways, laying down a combination of the paint colors.

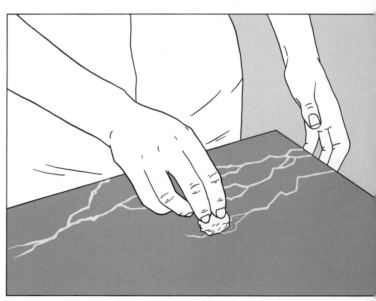

7 **Copying a crackled texture.** Use scissors to cut a piece of synthetic sponge about 1 inch long, ½ inch wide and ½ inch thick. Trim off the sharp edges and corners of the piece. Dip the sponge into the bowl of glaze and squeeze out the excess. Lightly press the sponge onto one of the wide patches of paint, then quickly lift it. The glaze will cause the paint it touches to separate, giving the area a cracked appearance.

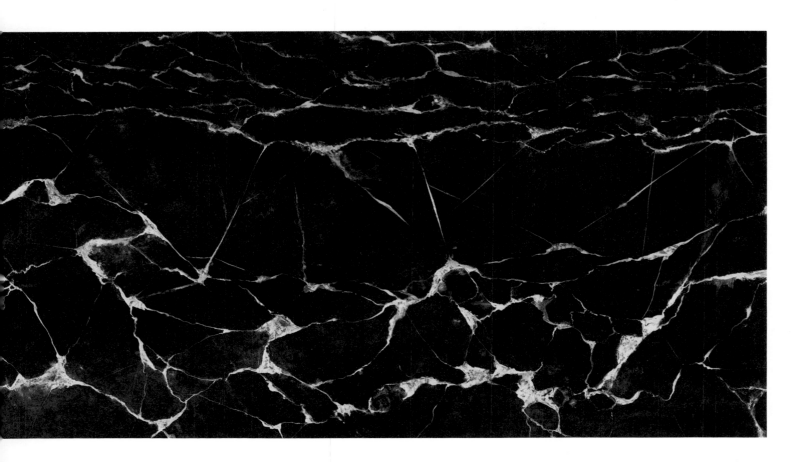

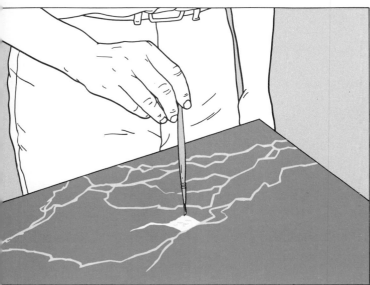

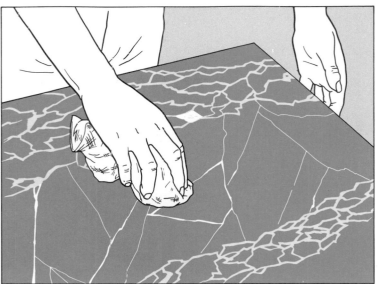

8 **Outlining a sponged area.** Dip the piece of sponge into the white paint and then into the surrounding glaze. Tap the sponge on a piece of newspaper until the paint leaves a soft, textured pattern. Then lightly press the sponge onto the furniture top at the end of a vein line. Rinse the sponge in mineral spirits and lay it aside. Dip a No. 1 artist's brush into the white paint and the surrounding glaze, and outline the sponged-on paint by lightly drawing a vein around its edge *(above)*.

9 **Softening the veins.** To create the straight, spidery veins that connect the two main pattern areas of the marble design — the narrowly spaced pattern at the top of the photograph above and the more widely spaced pattern at the bottom — dip a No. 0 artist's brush into the white paint and then into the surrounding glaze. Draw fine, straight veins that reach across the central area and connect with the veins and wide patches at the edges of the two patterns. Soften these lines — and any areas that appear harsh in color — by blotting them with a pad of clean, lint-free cloth, such as cheesecloth. Let the furniture top dry for 48 hours before varnishing it.

Simulated Rose Marble

Painting an imitation of rose marble like that in the one-third-scale photograph at left begins with applying a base of white semigloss alkyd enamel, then a coat of diluted shellac *(page 71, Step 1)*.

Three major colors and a veining color create the marble design. Squeeze into one dish a 1½-inch length (about 1½ teaspoons) of brown madder artist's oil paint, ½ inch of burnt sienna and inch of white. Mix the paints together with a palette knife.

In a second dish, mix together 1½ inches of brown madder and ½ inch of white oil paints. In a third dish, mix 1 inch of alizarin crimson and 1 inch of brown madder oil paints. In a fourth dish, mix the veining color — ½ inch each of brown madder and burnt umber oil paints.

Mix glaze *(box, page 75)* and pour it into a glass bowl. Apply a thin coat of the glaze to the furniture top *(page 75, Step 2)* before marbleizing it.

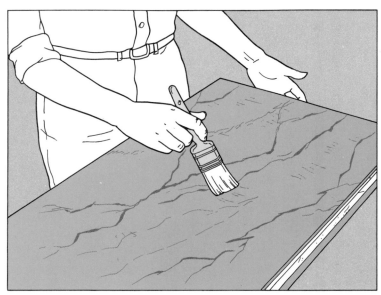

2 **Forming a variegated background.** Dip a No. 2 artist's brush into the veining color and hold it upright by the top of its handle; exert gentle pressure on the bristles while drawing a few heavy veins on the furniture top. Blot the veins with a pad of cheesecloth to soften the lines. Then stroke the entire surface lightly with a dry 2-inch natural-bristle brush *(above)* to blend the painted areas, remove some color and expose a little of the white background. Dip a small piece of sponge *(page 76, Step 7)* into the bowl of glaze. Pat the sponge on the surface in various areas to make the paint separate and appear cracked. Let the piece dry overnight before proceeding to Step 3.

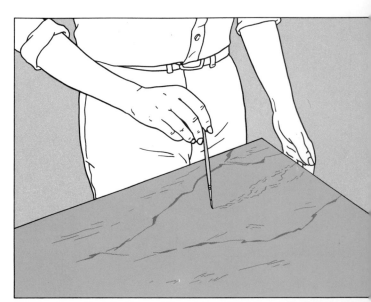

3 **Painting fine veins.** Squeeze a ¼-inch cylinder of brown madder oil paint into a flat dish or jar top. Add ½ teaspoon of glaze to the jar top; do not mix the paint and glaze. Dip a No. 1 artist's brush into the paint and then into the surrounding glaze. Hold the brush upright and lightly draw the bristle tips along the surface, lifting the brush at intervals to make tiny veins like those seen in the photograph above.

Brushing on the paint. Dip the tips of a 1-inch natural-bristle brush into any one of the three main colors. Exerting gentle pressure on the brush, scrub the paint across the surface in a curving, roughly diagonal strip about 6 to 8 inches wide. Use clean brushes of the same size and type to scrub on the remaining two colors so that the strips of paint slightly overlap *(right)*. Vary the juxtaposition of the colors and the width of each strip. When the surface is covered, blot with a cloth to soften the colors.

masking tape

4 **Making sprays of dots.** Dip the bristles of a clean, dry toothbrush into the brown paint and glaze prepared in Step 3. Holding the brush with the bristles toward the furniture top, pull your forefinger from front to back along the bristles to spatter dots of paint onto the surface. Let the furniture top dry for 48 hours, then varnish it.

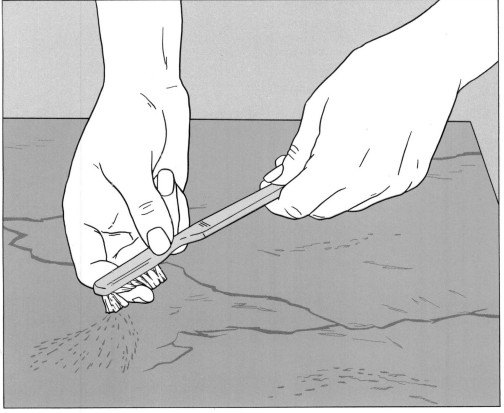

Simulated Carrara

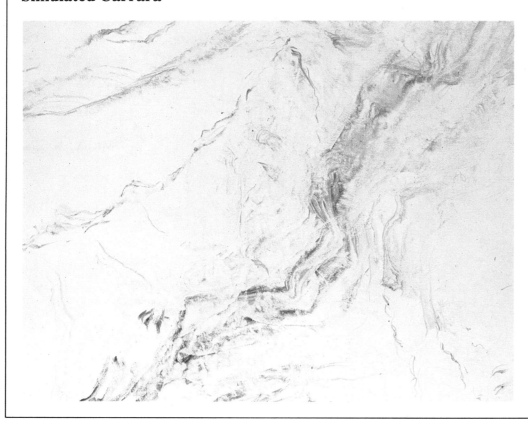

White carrara marble, as the one-third-scale photograph at left indicates, is subtly veined with gray. To simulate it, first apply a base coat of white semigloss alkyd enamel, and follow it with a coat of diluted shellac *(page 71, Step 1)*. Prepare glaze *(box, page 75)* and pour it into a glass bowl.

Squeeze a ½-inch length (about ½ teaspoon) of black oil paint into a flat dish or jar top; do not add any glaze. Using a foam-tipped applicator, glaze the furniture top *(page 75, Step 2)*. Next, dip the tip of a 1-inch natural-bristle brush into the glaze, then into the black paint; scrub this onto the furniture surface and blot it with a cloth *(page 75, Step 3)* to create a grayish background color. Then use a large artist's feather to pattern the furniture surface as shown at right.

Simulated Verde Antique

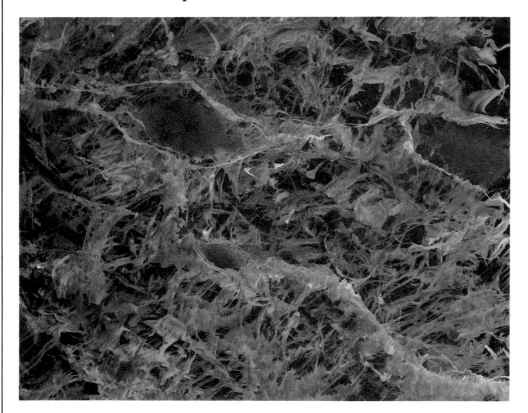

As the simulation in the one-half-scale photograph at left illustrates, verde antique — a green stone that is sold as marble — is characterized by many cloudy fossil areas and feathery markings. Here, marbleizing begins with a base of black semigloss alkyd enamel, followed by a coat of diluted shellac *(page 71, Step 1)*. Prepare glaze *(box, page 75)* and pour it into a glass bowl — but in this instance, do not apply glaze to the surface at the outset.

Squeeze a ½-inch length (about ½ teaspoon) of white oil paint into a flat dish or jar top. In a second dish, mix together ½ inch of viridian green and ½ inch of chromium oxide green. In a third, mix ¼ inch each of white, viridian green and chromium oxide green. Do not add glaze to the paints. Then follow the steps at right to paint the design.

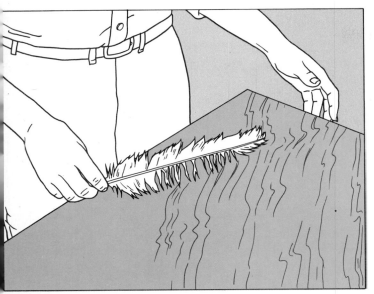

1 **Drawing feathery waves.** Holding a large artist's feather by the thick end of its quill, dip the edge of one side first into the bowl of glaze, then into the dish of black paint. Beginning at the edge of the furniture piece, lightly draw the feather diagonally across the furniture surface, making wavy lines that vary in width and length. Lay the feather aside and blot the wavy lines with a cheesecloth pad to soften their color.

2 **Drawing dark feathered lines.** Dip the tip of the feather first into the glaze, then into the black paint. Beginning at the edge, lightly pull the feather tip across the surface to create dark wavy veins across the lines made in Step 1. Blot the veins with the cheesecloth pad to soften their color. Clean the feather in mineral spirits and wipe it dry. Let the furniture piece dry for 48 hours before finishing it with varnish.

1 **Forming short, feathery lines.** Holding a large artist's feather by its quill, dip one long edge into the glaze, then into the mixture of viridian and chromium oxide green paints. Moving diagonally across the surface, repeatedly brush it with inch-long strokes. Clean the feather with mineral spirits and wipe it dry. Dip the feather's edge into the glaze and into the green-and-white paint mixture. Use the same motion to fill in unpainted areas and overlap previous strokes. Clean the feather and repeat the action to add white paint sparingly. Clean and dry the feather.

2 **Simulating fossil areas.** With a cheesecloth pad, lightly wipe away most of the freshly applied paint from one or two small patches on the furniture surface; leave just a hint of color there to simulate shadowy fossil areas. Dip the tip of the feather into the glaze and then into the white paint. With the tip of the feather, lightly paint a vein leading up to and around each fossil area. Then paint veins in other areas of the surface. Blot the veins, and any harsh areas of color, with the cloth. Let the surface dry for 48 hours, then apply varnish.

Simulated Travertine

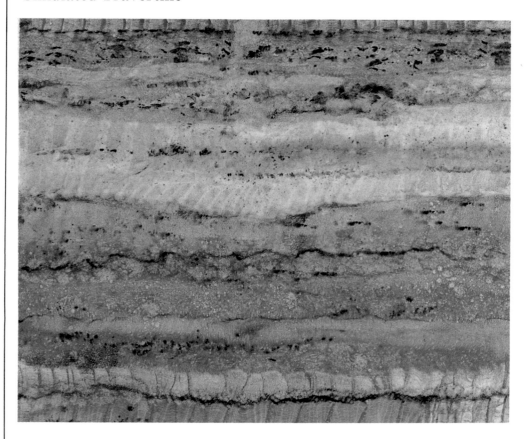

Travertine marble has a distinctive linear design that can be imitated by oil paint applied with pieces of sponge *(right)*. Cover a base of white semigloss alkyd enamel with a coat of diluted shellac *(page 71, Step 1)*. Prepare glaze *(box, page 75)* and pour it into a glass bowl.

Collect three flat dishes or jar tops. Into one dish squeeze ½ inch (about ½ teaspoon) each of burnt sienna and white oil paints. Into the second squeeze ½ inch each of burnt umber and white, and into the third squeeze ½ inch each of burnt sienna, burnt umber and white.

Add 2 teaspoons of glaze to each dish and stir each mixture with a palette knife. Then apply a thin coat of glaze to the furniture surface *(page 75, Step 2)*. Now follow the instructions below and at right to create an imitation of travertine like that seen in this one-quarter-scale photograph. When changing paint colors, clean the sponge by wiping it with a dry cloth, thus letting the colors mix somewhat for each new application.

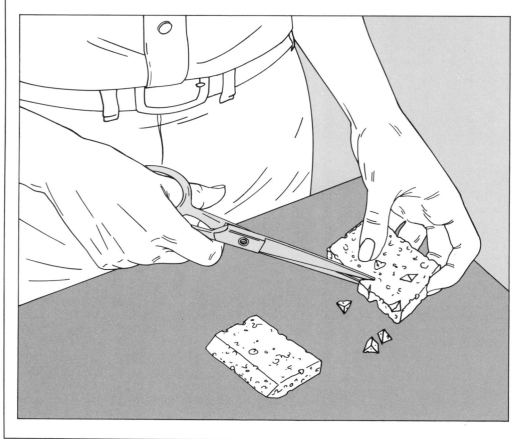

1 **Shaping the sponge.** Cut two pieces of sponge 3 inches by 2 inches by ½ inch. Use scissors to clip a long side of one of the pieces down to a thin beveled edge. Lay this sponge aside; it will be used only in Step 5. Then cut small chunks out of the faces and sides of the other sponge, enlarging some of its holes and creating jagged areas.

2 **Forming large blocks.** Pick up the sponge with holes cut into it. Dip about ⅓ of one of its wide surfaces into one paint color. Drag the sponge along as shown above, stopping and starting at roughly 1-inch intervals to create a blocklike pattern. Wipe the sponge with a cloth and use a different color to paint a wavy strip beside the first by wagging the sponge from side to side as you drag it along.

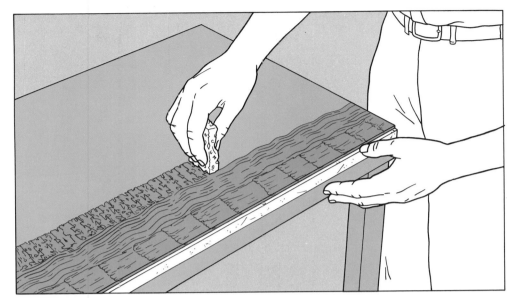

3 **Making small blocks.** Wipe the sponge on a cloth and dip its end into any one of the paints. Keeping the long edge of the sponge parallel to the already-painted strips, press the sponge onto the furniture surface. Then lift it, and press it to the surface again, placing each consecutive mark next to the previous one to create a continuous strip.

4 **Dabbing narrow strips.** Now wipe the sponge and load its end with another color. Turn it perpendicular to the last position so that it forms a narrower band as you dab it up and down. Varying colors and techniques, cover the surface with strips of paint; for some strips, load half the operative section of the sponge with one color and half with another. Next, pat glaze onto some areas *(page 76, Step 7)* with a clean sponge, and blot the surface with a cloth. Let the piece dry for 48 hours.

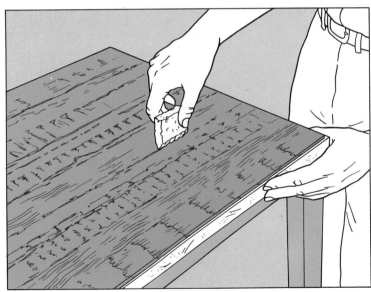

5 **Adding fine lines.** Squeeze a ½-inch length (about ½ teaspoon) of burnt umber oil paint into a dish; add 1 teaspoon of glaze and mix it in with a palette knife. Dip the beveled edge of the reserved sponge into the paint. Gently touch the beveled edge onto the surface to draw a series of thin, dark, broken lines between some pattern strips and down the face of others. Blot the fresh paint with a cloth to soften the colors, let it dry for 48 hours, then varnish.

Refined accents for bamboo furniture

Fanciful patterns of grass leaves, painted with artist's brushes, are a lovely finishing touch for almost any bamboo furniture, whether the real thing or — like the chair at right — wood carved to resemble bamboo.

This pattern consists of four basic elements — rings, blades of grass, dots and three-pronged leaf sprays — melded by a top coat of tinted antiquing glaze that reduces the contrast between the background color and the design. The kind and size of pattern element used varies with the size of the ringed joints on the furniture: At a small joint, only a ring is painted; at a medium-sized joint, a wider ring is augmented with grass blades and dots; at a large joint, a leaf spray is also added.

Because you will invert the piece as you work, remove any doors, drawers, drop leaves, loose shelves or other nonstructural parts; in the case of this chair, the upholstered slip seat is removed. If the piece is imitation bamboo, paint it with an overall color before decorating it; use an enamel undercoat and at least two coats of semigloss alkyd enamel in a color that will harmonize with your room's colors and those you have chosen for the leaves, rings and dots. Here, the background is yellowish white, the leaf decorations are green and the dots are red.

If you are working on genuine bamboo, remove old polish by rubbing the furniture well with a rag dipped in denatured alcohol. You need not apply background paint to real bamboo unless the clean surface is marred or discolored.

Finish preparing the surface by painting a protective band of 1-pound-cut white shellac *(page 42)*, extending about an inch above and below each joint. This clear band will allow you to correct mistakes in your design by wiping them away with a rag dampened with mineral spirits; the shellac keeps the mineral spirits from softening the background paint. Let the shellac dry for at least 30 minutes.

Apply the decorations in the sequence shown here, finishing with one kind before you start the next: Paint all of the rings before any leaf sprays, and so on. To reduce the danger of smearing the slow-drying paint, always start with the inmost parts of the furniture and work outward; use extra care when picking up the piece to move it as you work. And be sure to allow at least eight hours' drying time for each stage of the design.

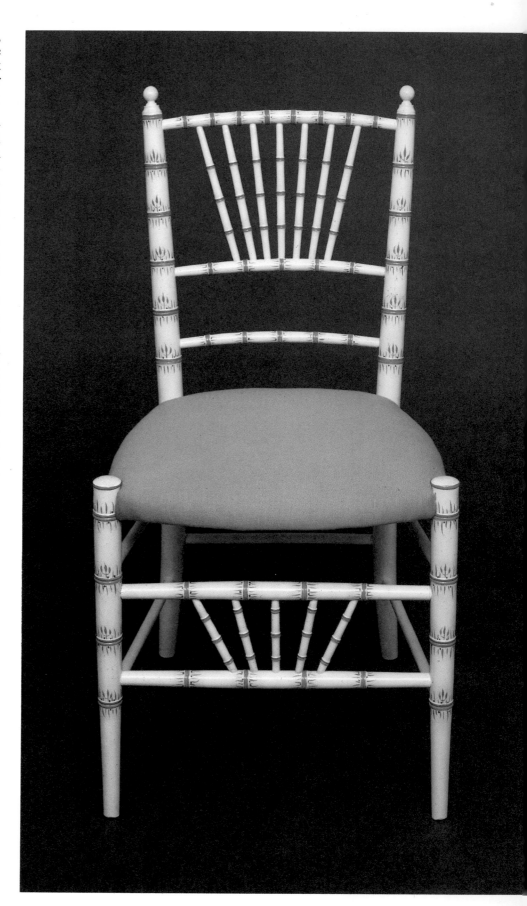

Mixing the green paint. In a clean glass container, prepare a transparent medium by mixing 1 tablespoon of semigloss alkyd varnish, 1 teaspoon of mineral spirits and ¼ teaspoon of japan drier. Add 1 teaspoon of sap green artist's oil paint to the medium, then use a clean spoon to stir the mixture well. Tie one thickness of old nylon stocking over the jar top, and strain the paint by pouring it into a clean glass jar equipped with an airtight lid. Cap the jar tightly until you are ready to use the paint. If the paint thickens as you work, thin it with a few drops of mineral spirits.

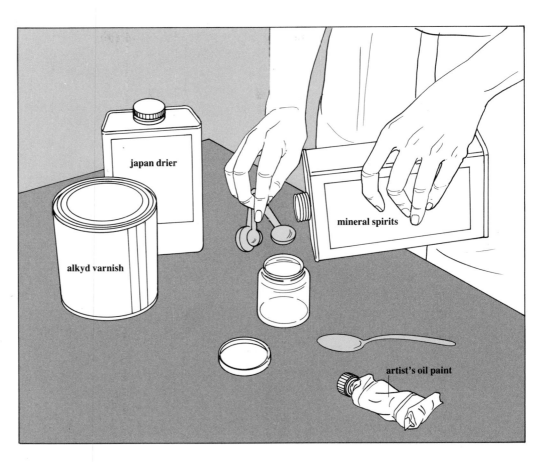

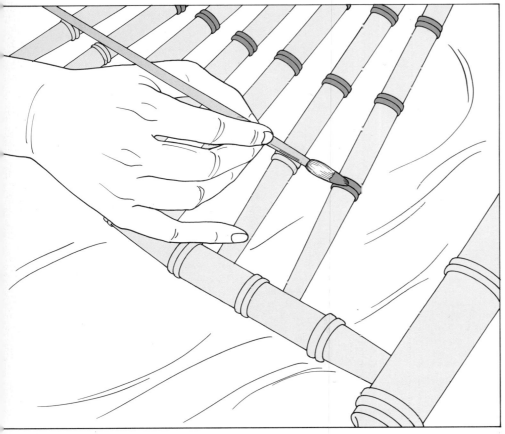

2 **Painting the rings.** Dip a No. 4 artist's brush into the green paint so its bristles are about half filled, then paint a ring about ¼ inch wide around one of the large bamboo joints. Steady your hand on the chair as you work, and move the chair as necessary so you can comfortably reach all sides of the joint. Paint similar rings to cover each joint — about ³⁄₁₆ inch for medium-sized joints and ⅛ inch for small joints — completing each ring before starting the next. Let the paint dry for eight hours before handling the chair for the next step. ▶

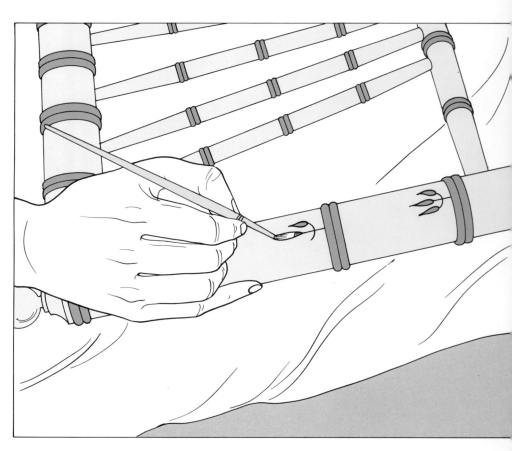

3 **Painting leaf sprays.** Lay the chair on its back. On the right front leg of the chair, paint a leaf spray *(box, opposite)* ascending from the front of the lowest ringed joint. Proceeding up the leg, paint a similar leaf spray at each joint, then on each joint of the other front leg. Working in the same manner, add leaf sprays on the front of the upright parts of the chair back, at each joint *(above)*. Let the paint dry for eight hours.

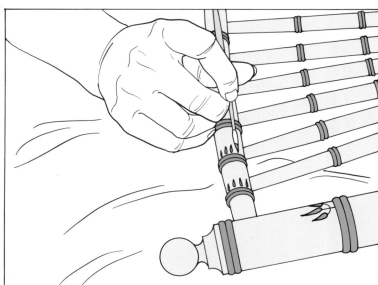

4 **Painting grass blades.** Use a No. 1 artist's brush to paint a band of grass blades on the near side of the joint farthest from you on the top rail. Start each blade about ¹⁄₁₆ inch from the joint and draw the brush toward you, using the brush technique you used on the leaves to vary the width of each blade. Space the blades ⅛ to ¼ inch apart, and vary the lengths randomly, between ¼ and ⅝ inch. Paint bands of blades next to all but the smallest joints, working from farthest to nearest. When the paint has dried, work in a similar manner to paint a band on the other side of each joint. On joints that have a leaf spray, place the first grass blade next to the spray and work around the joint to the other side of the spray. Let the paint dry for eight hours.

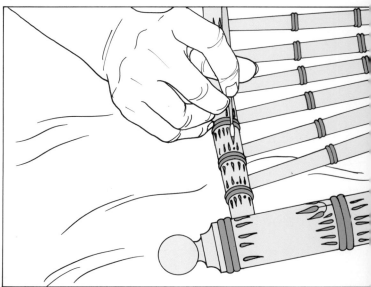

5 **Adding red dots.** Mix red paint, following the instructions in Step 1 but substituting 1 teaspoon of vermilion oil paint for the green paint. Wet the tip of a No. 1 artist's brush with the paint mixture and use it to paint a ¹⁄₁₆-inch dot between two grass blades, about ¹⁄₁₆ inch from the joint. Paint similar dots at irregular intervals between the grass blades, painting six to eight dots at a medium-sized joint and 12 to 15 at a large one.

A Calligraphic Technique for Drawing Leaf Sprays

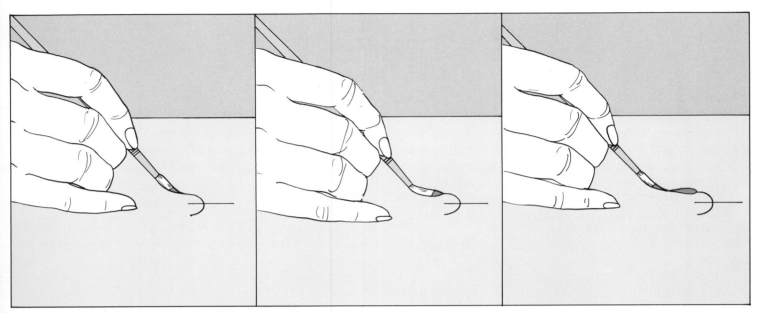

Painting leaves of variable width. Dip a No. 2 artist's brush ¼ inch into green paint. Pressing very lightly, paint three narrow stems with three separate strokes *(above, left)*. Then make a leaf at the end of each stem: Touch the brush tip to the top of the stem, and press the brush against the surface to spread the bristles *(above, center)* to the maximum width of the leaf. Next draw the brush toward you while lifting it, so that only the tip still touches the surface when the brush has moved ½ inch *(above, right)*. Finish the leaf by lifting the brush completely away.

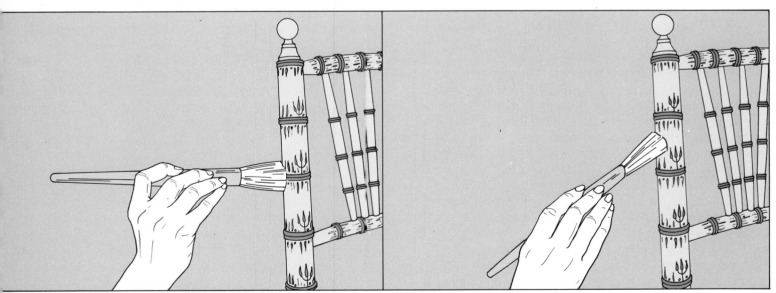

6 **Applying antiquing glaze.** Mix a transparent glaze medium by combining 2 teaspoons of japan drier and 4 teaspoons each of mineral spirits, boiled linseed oil and semigloss alkyd varnish. Tint the medium with 1 teaspoon each of sap green and raw umber oil paint. Stir the glaze well and strain it through nylon *(Step 1)* into a glass jar that has an airtight cap.

Work with only a teaspoon of the glaze at a time, set out in a glass bowl. Dip a 2-inch sash brush into the glaze, wetting the bottom ⅛ inch of the bristles. Stroke the brush back and forth on a clean paper towel, moving to a new spot every few strokes, until the brush leaves only a faint smudge of glaze. Apply glaze over a decorated joint by repeated-ly tapping the tips of the brush bristles lightly against the surface *(above, left)*. Apply glaze over all of the joints in one section of the chair — one rung or one leg, for example; each time you reload the brush, work out most of the glaze. Then, as soon as you finish with the joints, immediately apply glaze to the undecorated parts of that section of the chair, us-ing light, lengthwise strokes *(above, right)*, but loading the brush in the same way. Replenish the glaze in the bowl with fresh glaze from the jar as necessary, and glaze the rest of the chair, finishing an entire sec-tion before starting on the next. Let the glaze dry for at least eight hours, then coat the entire chair with semigloss alkyd varnish *(pages 44-45)*.

Veneers: Wood's beauty in thin slices

For many people, veneer on furniture seems a cheap deception, since the thin layer of superior wood conceals less expensive material beneath. But in fact veneer is essential to the creation of many highly desirable decorative effects and has graced some of the most beautiful and valuable products of the furniture maker's art for the last 5,000 years.

It is true that the ancient Egyptians developed veneer for reasons of economy. Because there were few forests in Egypt, the pharaohs' craftsmen were encouraged to slice rare woods as thin as possible. By the 18th Century, however, European artisans were employing veneer as a matter of choice, for the creative possibilities it presented. They lavishly adorned veneered furniture with intricate pictorial inlays of precious woods; one exquisitely veneered roll-top desk made for King Louis XV of France took fully nine years to complete.

Today, for reasons of both economy and beauty, the use of veneer is more widespread than ever. And, thanks to the development of modern adhesives, successful veneering is no longer the exclusive franchise of professional craftsmen. Contact cement bonds veneer instantly and thus obviates the extensive clamping that is necessary when veneer is applied with liquid hide glue made from animal hides and bones (*page 102*).

People restoring their own furniture can apply veneers on smooth surfaces with little more effort than it takes to produce any other finish. This chapter details the necessary techniques, from laying down a simple veneer to forming veneer patterns and inlaying a design. The chapter ends with demonstrations of wood veneer repairs, and an explanation of how to cover a furniture top with another kind of veneer — leather.

There are some 200 different varieties of veneer, ranging from familiar walnut and cherry to exotic light satinwood and rare ebony, available for use in veneering at home. Lumberyards, woodworking-supply stores and mail-order suppliers sell veneers and inlays, as well as the necessary specialized tools, including veneer saws (*page 92, Step 5*). Some mail-order houses offer extensive catalogues and sell boxes of small veneer samples that are invaluable in making selections.

Buyers should know that veneers differ not only by tree species, but also by the way logs are cut; two sheets of veneer from the same kind of tree have very different appearances if they are sliced by different methods. Flat, or plain-sliced, veneer (*opposite, top right*) is cut in parallel longitudinal slices from a log sawed lengthwise in half. The sheets are 12 to 18 inches wide and have the same variegated grain configuration as a board of lumber. Quarter-sliced veneer is cut from a lengthwise quarter section of a log; the blade strikes the tree's growth rings at a 45° angle so that the veneer, 4 to 12 inches wide, is striped by straight, narrow grain lines (*opposite, middle right*). Rotary-cut veneer is sliced from a turning log like paper being unwound from a roll. The wide continuous sheet that results has sharply varied grain markings (*opposite, bottom right*).

Other grain patterns are produced by taking veneer not from the trunk, but from special sections of the tree. The fork area where a large branch joins the trunk yields crotch veneer, with swirling grain figures caused by twisted wood fibers (*opposite, top left*). A burl — a large bump created by cell growth in response to an injury — renders a veneer characterized by swirls and knots (*opposite, middle left*). From the bottom of the tree comes butt, or stump, wood (*opposite, bottom left*), with a compressed grain pattern marked by ripples. Veneers from these areas, cut by plain slicing, prove narrow but, like all veneer sheets, can easily be joined to form wider panels (*pages 91-92, Steps 3-5*).

As sheets are taken from the log portion, called a flitch, they are kept in the original cutting order. The assembled package of veneer, also known as a flitch, is sold as a unit or in consecutive sheets. Because each sheet in a flitch is nearly identical to the previous one in grain figure, pairs can be matched in mirror images to create arresting designs (*pages 96-99*).

The many faces of wood. All but one of the veneers opposite are cut from the same wood: walnut. (The rotary-cut veneer at bottom, far right, is birch; highly valued walnut is not often used for this inexpensive cut.) The grain patterns at near right come from different parts of the tree; those at far right result from slicing the trunk by different methods.

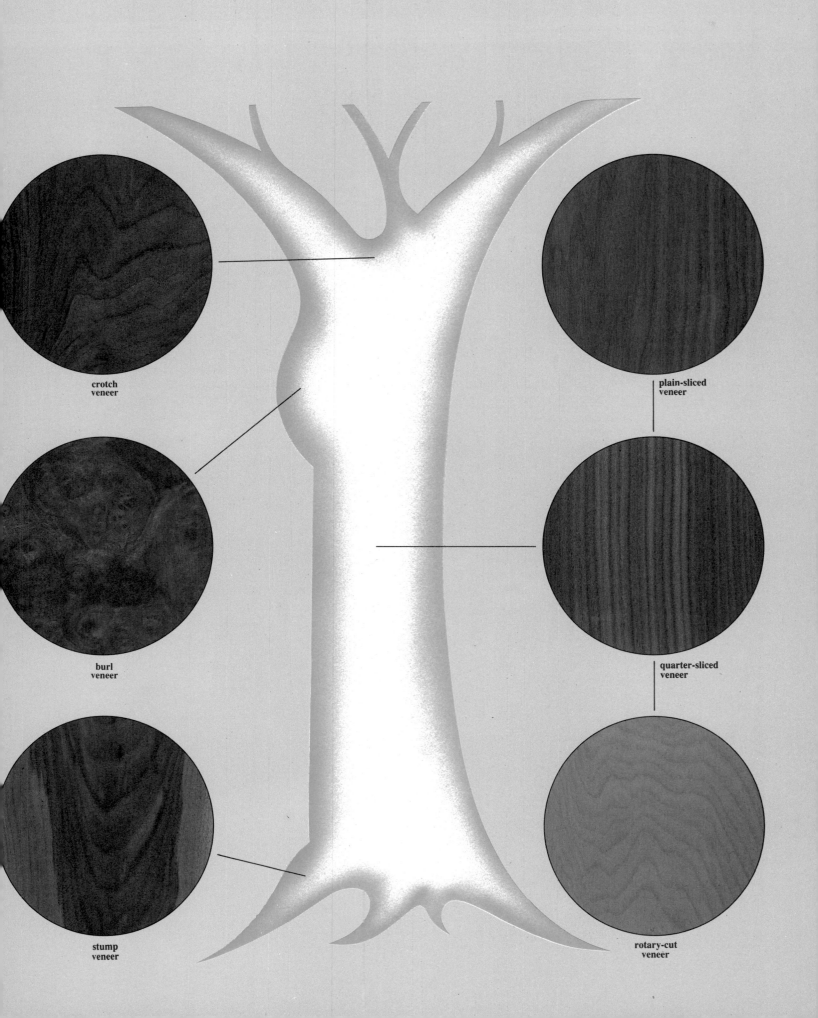

crotch
veneer

burl
veneer

stump
veneer

plain-sliced
veneer

quarter-sliced
veneer

rotary-cut
veneer

A primer of application procedures

The top of a table, the face of a headboard, the front of a cabinet door — any flat surface with straight edges is a prime candidate for veneering. The surface may be solid wood, plywood or particleboard; it may be unfinished or previously finished or veneered. But it must be absolutely smooth: Veneers are only $\frac{1}{28}$ inch to $\frac{1}{60}$ inch thick, so even minute bumps and dents will show through. And it must be flat; the sheets cannot be wrapped around curves and beveled edges.

Old finishes must be sanded with fine (150-grit) paper if they are in good condition; otherwise, they should be stripped off (pages 34-35). Fractured veneer and the glue under it must be removed (pages 115-116, Steps 1-3). Dents and holes must be filled (pages 120-121). For ease of handling, furniture should be disassembled as completely as possible: Remove doors, drawers, glass and mirrored parts. Detach a tabletop from its base and take off any hinged leaves.

Veneers are sold by the square foot in 3-foot to 8-foot lengths; widths vary from 4 to 12 or more inches. To determine how much veneer you need for a rectangular object, multiply the width in inches by the length in inches; for a circular object simply square the diameter; and for an oval, multiply the two different diameters. Divide these totals by 144 to translate square inches into square feet. Allow about one third extra for matching the grain patterns in the wood: Veneer sheets are generally inexpensive, so the excess will not be prohibitive.

While veneer is being sliced, the two sides of the sheet develop different characteristics. The leading edge of the beveled knife blade used for slicing (Step 2, inset) compresses the wood on one side to achieve a smooth surface. At the same time, the blade mars the other surface with minuscule cracks, called checks; the result is a somewhat rough surface. Before you begin working with a sheet of veneer, test it as demonstrated opposite; the smooth, so-called compression side is preferable as the face of your veneer.

Because of veneer's narrow width, you will need to butt sheets and tape the joints, until you get the desired width. Then you can work with the panel as if it were a single piece. Make a paper template of the shape to be covered, cut the veneer to fit, then apply it to the surface with contact cement for a lasting bond.

The proper tool for cutting straight lines is a veneer saw, available at lumberyards and mail-order houses. But a utility knife with a sharp blade can be used to make straight cuts — and is the best tool for curved lines. Other tools needed are a chisel to make short cuts — a chisel with a 2-inch-wide blade is best — C clamps to fasten a straightedge against a cutting line, inexpensive paintbrushes to spread contact cement, a hand roller to bond the cement, paper or masking tape to hold sections together, and fine (150-grit) and very-fine (220-grit) sandpaper.

When you have bonded and sanded the veneer, you can apply the finish of your choice. If you use a penetrating oil finish, experiment first with scraps of veneer cemented to a board: Some oil finishes soften contact cement.

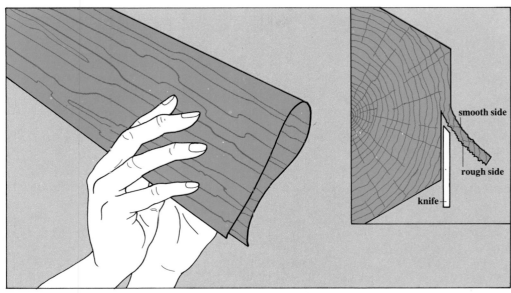

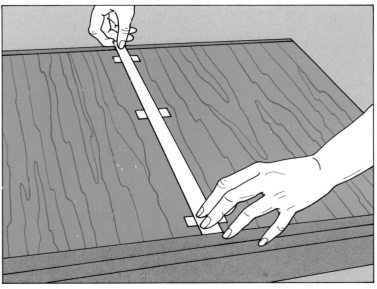

1 **Making a template.** Unroll enough brown wrapping paper on a flat work surface to accommodate the object — in this case a 24-by-30-inch tabletop. If necessary, tape two lengths of paper together to provide the size required. Place the tabletop face down on the paper. Then trace around the top, holding a pencil perpendicular to the paper rather than at an angle so the pattern will be about ⅛ inch larger all around. Remove the tabletop and cut the pattern with scissors.

2 **Finding the smooth side of veneer.** Bend a sheet of veneer in half along the grain, first in one direction, then in the other, to identify the smooth side that was created by the leading edge of the blade as it cut the veneer (inset). When the smooth side is on the outside, it will resist bending and make a cracking sound; when the rough side is outside, it will bend easily without audible cracking (above). Use the smooth side as the veneer's face, placing it upward on the work surface. Sometimes a sheet of veneer may flex equally to either side; then you can work with either side.

3 **Planning a seam.** The mahogany veneer shown here is 12½ inches wide; thus the best place for a seam on the 24-by-30-inch oval table is the center. For narrower-width veneers, plan two or more seams, placed equidistant from the edges. Slide the sheets back and forth — smooth side up — until the two form a pleasing, continuous grain pattern.

4 **Taping the sections.** Overlap the edges of the veneer at the seam by ¼ inch. Tear strips of ½-inch-wide paper tape or masking tape about 3 inches long and fasten them at right angles to the seam, near each of its ends and in the middle. Run one long strip of tape along the whole seam (above). Tape any cracks on the ends of the sheets to prevent further splitting while handling the veneer. ▶

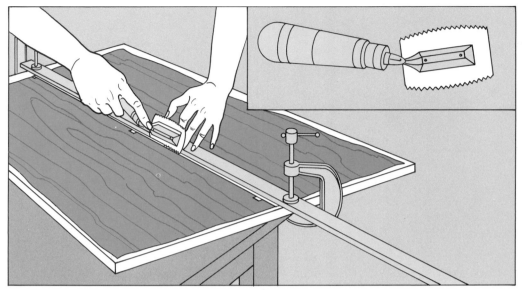

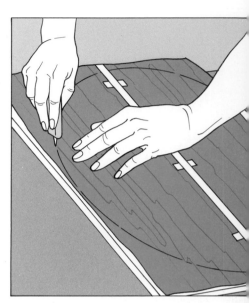

5 **Preparing the seam for a butt joint.** Place the veneer on a piece of plywood or any other surface suitable for cutting. Center a straightedge — such as a metal yardstick — on the overlap and fasten it with C clamps at each end. Using the straightedge as a guide, cut through the tape and veneer with a veneer saw *(inset)*. Apply moderate pressure on the saw, and cut on the draw stroke. It may take several passes to cut through both layers of veneer, but sawing the two sheets at once will ensure a tight joint that makes the seam almost invisible. Remove the tape from the seam. If the edges of the cut look fuzzy, lightly sand with fine (150-grit) sandpaper. Butt the two sheets, and tape the joint again as in Step 4. The tape should be on the upper face of the veneer.

6 **Cutting the veneer for the tabletop.** Crease the template in half lengthwise, then unfold the template and tape it to the veneer, matching the center-line fold with the seam at both ends. Using a No. 2 pencil or felt-tipped pen, outline the pattern on the veneer. Remove the template. Then cut lightly along the outline with a utility knife to score the oval *(above)*. Cut a second time to slice through the veneer.

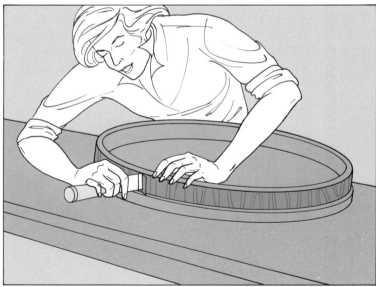

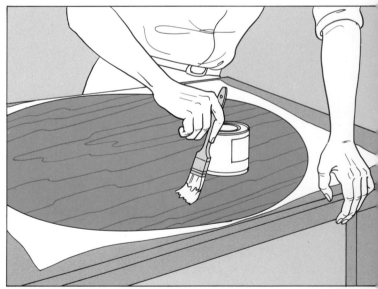

10 **Fitting the skirt.** Tape one end of the veneer onto the table's skirt and wrap the band tightly around the skirt, letting the veneer overlap at the end. With a pencil, mark a line on the overlapping strip at the end of the lower strip. Then, applying steady pressure on a sharp 2-inch-wide chisel, sever the veneer along the line in one clean cut. Or, remove the band from the skirt and cut it at your worktable, using a straightedge and veneer saw or knife.

Measure the thickness of the table's edge and add a ⅛-inch margin; measure the circumference and calculate the number of strips needed as in Step 7, allowing for ¼-inch overlaps. Cut out a band of veneer, repeating the techniques in Steps 7 through 10.

11 **Applying the adhesive.** With a tack rag, dust the tabletop and the top panel of veneer. Using a clean 2-inch nylon-bristle brush, coat the back side of the veneer with a solvent-based contact cement, spreading it in a thin, smooth layer. Next spread contact cement on the tabletop, repeating the careful brushing over the entire top. Wrap the brush in foil to keep it from hardening before the next coat. Let the cement dry to the touch, as the manufacturer directs, about 15 to 30 minutes. As soon as the cement feels dry and a piece of brown wrapping paper will not stick to it, apply a second coat to the veneer and the tabletop. Let them dry for about an hour.

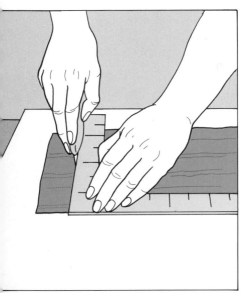

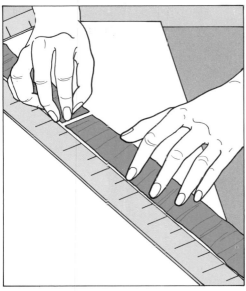

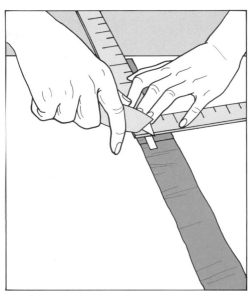

7 **Cutting the table's skirt.** Measure the height of the skirt and add ⅛ inch for a margin. Measure the skirt's circumference and divide this figure by the width of your veneer to calculate how many pieces you need; cut one or two extra to allow for a ¼-inch overlap at each end of every piece. Place the veneer on the cutting surface, and mark off successive strips of the necessary height; use a carpenter's square to guide a utility knife for cutting the veneer.

8 **Connecting the pieces.** Line up two veneer strips for the table's skirt against the edge of the carpenter's square. Position the strips end to end and overlap the seam where they meet by ¼ inch. Tape the strips together with a 2-inch length across the seam and a full-length strip of paper tape or masking tape to cover the entire seam. Continue adding veneer strips in this manner until you have made a band of all the veneer pieces.

9 **Preparing for butt joints.** To achieve tight-fitting seams, cut through both pieces of veneer at each taped overlap, guiding the utility knife along the carpenter's square as in Step 5. Butt the veneer strips tightly at each joint, and tape them together again.

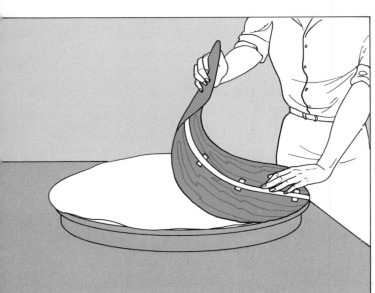

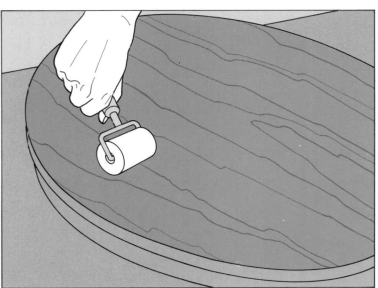

12 **Bonding the veneer.** Place a piece of brown wrapping paper — the paper template made in Step 1 is ideal — on the adhesive-coated tabletop; at this stage, the contact cement will only stick to contact cement. Position the veneer on top of the paper, adhesive side down. Make sure to leave an even margin all around. When you are satisfied that the veneer is positioned perfectly, lift one edge and with the other hand gently pull a section of the paper away without disturbing the veneer, joining the two adhesive surfaces. Carefully pushing toward the opposite edge of the veneer and flattening the veneer with your hand as you proceed, gradually pull out all of the paper to bond the veneer to the tabletop.

13 **Rolling the veneer.** Immediately smooth the surface with a hand roller, working in the direction of the grain and applying firm and even pressure. Go over the tabletop several times to eliminate any air pockets and to ensure good adhesion. ▶

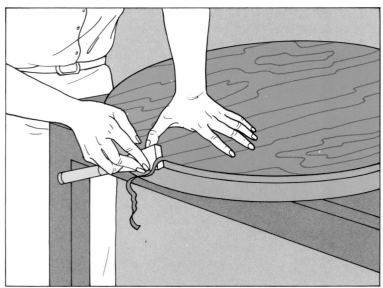

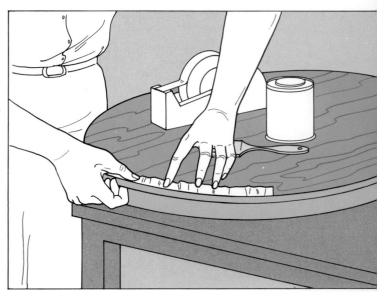

14 **Trimming the edge.** Holding the back of the chisel's blade flush against the edge of the table, cut through the overhanging veneer — pushing the blade in short strokes as you slice. The bond between tabletop and veneer will keep the edge from splitting. Then sand lightly, using fine (150-grit) sandpaper until the edge is smooth.

15 **Installing the edge band.** Mask the outer rim of the tabletop with tape *(above)* to prevent contact cement from marring the surface. With a clean, narrow paintbrush, apply contact cement to the table edge and the thin band of veneer, using the technique in Step 11. When the cement has dried to the touch, position the band with your hand — the top flush with the tabletop, the margin overhanging the bottom. Immediately roll the band with a hand roller until you are sure that the bond is tight. Trim the bottom of the band with a chisel and sandpaper as described in Step 14. Remove the tape.

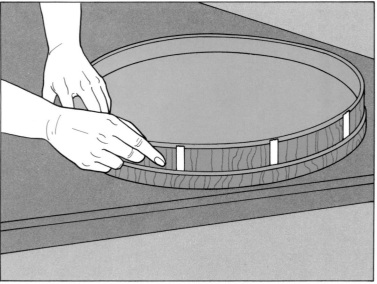

16 **Placing the skirt.** Turn the tabletop upside down and prepare the skirt and its veneer band with contact cement as described in Step 11. Pressing the top of the band against the underside of the tabletop, place the band around the skirt. Bond the veneer, using the technique described in Step 15, and trim the overhang.

17 **Sanding the surface.** Inspect the veneer surfaces to make sure they are smooth. If you find a blister, cover it with a terry-cloth towel and place an iron, set to medium, on top for a minute or so; heat will soften the contact cement so you can level the area with a hand roller again. Use a sheet of fine (150-grit) sandpaper, folded into quarters, to lightly sand the arris — the joint where the two veneer surfaces meet at the tabletop's rim — until the edges blend together. Then sand all veneer surfaces by hand with fine sandpaper. Always move with the grain. As soon as the surface looks even, change to very-fine (220-grit) paper to remove any hairline scratches so the wood feels smooth and silky. Finish the wood.

Ready-made Veneer Faces

Matched faces of richly figured veneer, such as those on the tabletop below, are available already assembled by mail order from veneer specialists. They range from the radial-matched walnut veneer shown here to olive-ash burls in sunburst design, fancy walnut crotch patterns, exotic wood combinations of ebony and maple, even inlaid chess and backgammon designs. Made for 30-inch to 33-inch round tops, 24-inch squares, and rectangles of 15 by 30 inches — or multiples thereof — such veneer faces can be applied to a piece of furniture of suitable size with a minimum of effort.

These veneer faces arrive with the grain matched at seams that are already taped together *(inset, below)*. You apply the veneer in the same way as any other, by cementing it to its base *(Steps 11-13)*. For tables, edge bands in rolls of 1 inch by 8 feet are ample to encircle a 30-inch-wide top. After being trimmed and sanded *(Steps 14 and 17)*, the new surface needs only to be finished by one of the techniques that are described on pages 36-45.

Pleasing patterns from matched figures

Strongly figured sheets of veneer bearing nearly identical grain patterns can be cut and fitted together with dramatic results: A four-way match of walnut crotch veneer graces the tabletop below, and diagonal layouts of straight-grained veneer create the diamond patterns on page 99. Such combinations are possible because in a flitch — a bundle of consecutively cut sheets of veneer — each sheet nearly duplicates the grain of the previous sheet.

Positioning two consecutive sheets as if they were the opened pages of a book results in a mirror image and is called book-matching. Book-matched patterns consisting of four or more sections can look especially attractive when they involve the swirling grain figures of crotch, burl or stump wood *(page 89)* — produced as wood fibers are thickened and twisted during the growth of the tree.

Any pattern with a mirror image uses what is known as the compression side of one sheet of veneer and what is called the tension side of the other *(page 91, Step 2)*. On many veneers, the compression side is noticeably smoother than the tension side. Before creating a mirror image, test the veneer by flexing it along the grain: Only well-cut sheets that bend almost equally easily to either side will provide sufficiently smooth surfaces on both sides.

Crotch, burl and stump veneers often arrive in a buckled condition, because of the tension in the twisted fibers. When using these veneers you must first press the sheets flat *(opposite, Steps 1 and 2)*; the pressing process requires many C clamps — at least a dozen for these 12-by-36-inch sheets — and some heavy object to serve as press weights.

In addition, you will need a veneer saw *(page 92, Step 5)* and a utility knife for cutting, and a straightedge. Other tools required are a carpenter's square, to attain perfect 90° corners; masking tape to hold veneer sections together; disposable brushes and contact cement for adhering the veneer to the furniture; and fine (150-grit) and very-fine (220-grit) sandpaper for finishing. If you are creating a diamond design, you will also need a plastic drafting triangle that has a 30° angle and a 60° angle or two 45° angles.

For patterns using both sides of veneer, the best finish is one that will seal the rougher, tension side: a lacquer or varnish in multiple coats.

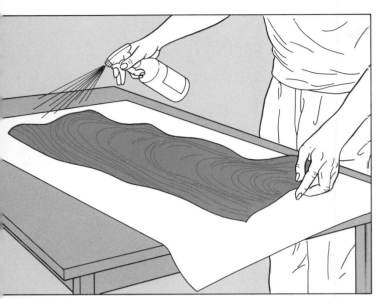

1 **Dampening buckled veneer.** Place a buckled sheet of veneer over a piece of brown wrapping paper set on a flat worktable. Dampen the veneer with a fine mist of water from a spray bottle. Rub the sheet with your hands to make sure the water penetrates the veneer evenly. Do not soak the veneer. Turn the sheet over and dampen the other side. Spray three more sheets of veneer from the same flitch and stack them, sandwiching each sheet between four pieces of wrapping paper. The paper will absorb the moisture as the veneer dries.

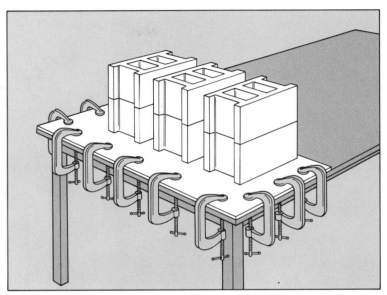

2 **Pressing the veneer.** Flatten the sandwiched stack of veneer and paper with a sheet of plywood, and clamp it to the worktable with C clamps placed every 6 inches along the edges, tightening the clamps hard to exert maximum pressure. Now load bricks, cinder blocks, heavy books or bodybuilding weights everywhere on the plywood that the clamps do not reach. Check the veneer after 24 hours; it should be dry and flat. If it still curls, dampen the sheets again and sandwich each one between fresh pieces of paper for another 24 to 48 hours — however long it takes to make the veneer completely flat and dry. Then proceed with the job immediately; the veneer may curl up again within a few hours.

3 **Making a template.** Cover the surface to be veneered — in this case, a tabletop — with a slightly larger piece of paper. Smooth the paper from the center to the rim on all sides, pushing the excess up and against the rim. Then, holding the paper in place with one hand, run a fingernail or a pencil along the bottom edge of the rim to mark the tabletop's outline on the paper. (For a surface without a rim, crease the excess paper down over the edges.) Cut the paper template and test it for fit. Make any adjustments necessary: You need an exact replica of the tabletop. Now, aligning the edges precisely, fold the template lengthwise in half, then crosswise in quarters. ▶

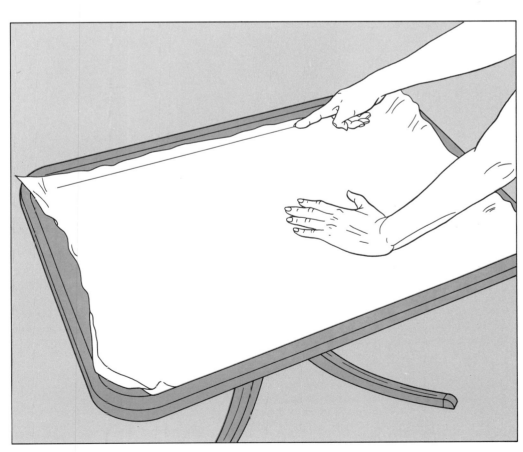

4 **Selecting a focal point.** Trace the quarter-folded template onto a sheet of paper or cardboard, and draw a 1-inch border around it. Cut along the inner lines and around the outside of the border. Then use the resulting frame as a viewer on a sheet of veneer. Move the viewer across the veneer *(left)*, seeking the section most worthy of repetition in mirror images. Look for a pronounced grain figure that will provide a dramatic focal point at the junction of the four pieces and that also will be completed by swirls extending to the edge of the viewer. You can test how an area will look in mirror image by holding a hand mirror perpendicular to the veneer on an inner edge of the viewer. When you have decided what section you want to use, place the quarter-folded template over that area and, with a pencil, trace its two straight edges onto the veneer.

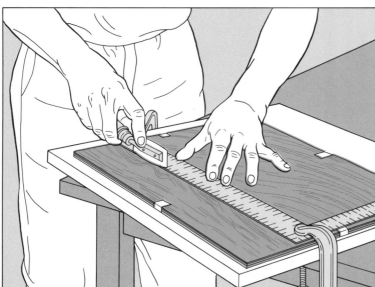

5 **Cutting the center lines.** Stack the four veneer sheets on a cutting surface with the marked sheet on top, making sure the grain patterns align. Tape the edges so the sheets cannot shift. Cutting one sheet at a time with a veneer saw against a straightedge, trim the stack to a manageable length; allow at least a 1-inch margin outside the traced lines. Tape the newly cut edges. Now align the outside edges of a carpenter's square with the two straight lines traced from the template's folded sides in Step 4, and hold it in position with two C clamps. Cut along the square's outside edges with the pleasing veneer saw, one sheet at a time. These cut edges will form the center lines of the completed panel.

6 **Cutting the panel to size.** Remove the tape from the stack of veneer and arrange the four cut pieces as they will appear on the tabletop. Butt the edges together tightly and fasten them with tape *(page 92, Step 5)*. Unfold the template and lay it on the veneer panel, matching the fold lines to the taped seams of the veneer. Tape the template in position, trace its outline with a pencil and then remove the template. Cut along the pencil line with a utility knife *(page 92, Step 6)*. Check the fit of the completed panel against the tabletop. Now fix the veneer to the tabletop with contact cement *(pages 92-93, Steps 11-13)*, and sand and finish the table *(page 94, Step 17)*.

Geometric Designs from Stripes

1 Positioning the template. When using straight-grained veneer to create diamond or reverse-diamond patterns *(below)*, make a paper template of the surface to be veneered, and fold the template in quarters. Align the short side of a 30°/60° drafting triangle with the edge of the veneer sheet or taped-together veneer panel. Now position the template against the triangle's hypotenuse, as shown above. (If you want a squared diamond rather than an elongated one, use a 45°/45° triangle instead of the 30°/60° triangle.)

2 Tracing the template. Draw the outline of the template with a pencil. Then align the template with one side of the penciled rectangle and trace it again. Trace the template twice more, so that you have four rectangles *(above)*. Now, on a cutting board, cut out the rectangles with a utility knife held against a carpenter's square *(opposite, Step 5)*, shifting the square as necessary to make sure that every corner of each rectangle is a 90° angle and that all the edges are straight.

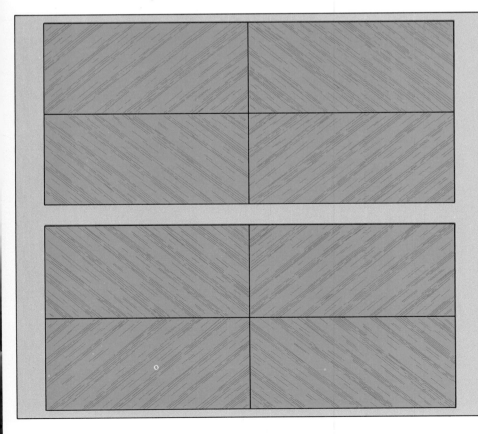

3 Arranging the pattern. To form a diamond, position the four sections as in the top picture at left; the upper right and lower left sections have their smooth, compression surfaces up, and the other two sections are reversed to show their rougher, tension surfaces. To produce a reverse diamond *(bottom picture at left)*, turn all the pieces over so that each reveals the surface that was facing down in the diamond arrangement. When you have the design you want, butt and tape the sections together *(page 92, Step 5)* and apply the completed panel to the furniture *(pages 92-93, Steps 11-13)*. Sand and finish the wood.

Introducing a decorative highlight

Inlays of rare woods, shaped and set to detailed perfection, once were the work solely of master craftsmen. Today, only a modicum of skill is required to achieve the same effect — by applying ready-made inlays that can be purchased from most veneer suppliers. Medallions, such as that in the mahogany table at right, and strips, like those inlaid in the teak butler's table on page 103, are available in many patterns.

When selecting a combination of veneer and inlay, make sure the wood colors are complementary and the surrounding veneer provides an appropriately muted background; a richly figured veneer detracts from an elaborate inlay.

To fit an inlay into a surface that is already veneered, you can cut through the veneer with a utility knife, scrape out the recess as you would when patching (page 116, Step 3), then glue the inlay into the opening. The easiest way to install an inlay, however, is to fit it into a new panel of veneer and then apply the two together to the furniture. The technique for applying an inlay medallion is described on the next two pages; instructions for inlaying strips begin on page 103.

An inlay medallion comes from the supplier set into a small piece of veneer to guard its edges, its face glued to a sheet of paper for protection. When you are ready to begin, cut the scrap veneer and excess paper from the edges of the medallion, leaving intact the paper glued to its face.

Inlays come in thicknesses of $1/20$ and $1/28$ inches, whereas most veneer sheets are $1/32$ inch thick. So you must sand the inlay down to the level of the veneer (Step 5) after fixing both in place with contact cement. If you are working on a small, flat surface such as the tabletop at right, you might be able to use hide glue instead of contact cement. Hide glue is slower to bond than contact cement, and it thus allows more time to position the veneer. However, special clamps are required to hold veneer and inlay in place while the glue dries (box, page 102). The clamping process makes it possible to use hide glue only if veneer and inlay are of equal thickness.

In either case you will need cutting tools (a veneer saw, a utility knife and a chisel), a paintbrush for applying adhesive, and fine-pointed veneer pins, which do not leave visible holes, to hold the medallion in position.

1 **Centering the medallion.** Cut out and tape together a panel of veneer for the tabletop as described on pages 91-92, Steps 1-6. Lay the panel face up on a sheet of plywood or other cutting board, and place the medallion — its paper-covered face up — on the taped seam, roughly in the middle of the panel. (If it is important to orient the top of the inlay design in a particular direction on your piece of furniture, and if you cannot see the inlay's face through the paper, look at the unpapered reverse.) Now measure the distances from each end and from the sides of the panel, to position the medallion exactly in the center. When you are sure the medallion is centered, push veneer pins through it and into the cutting board to hold it in place.

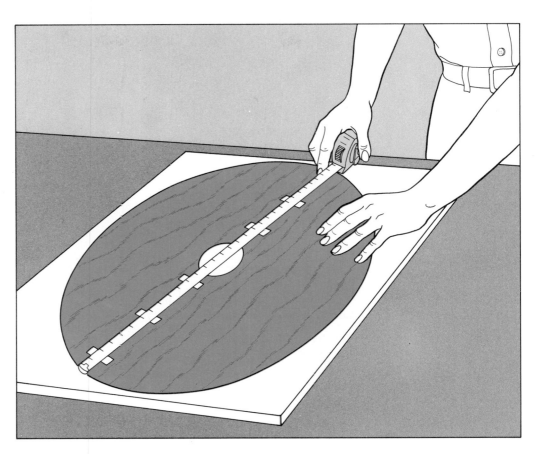

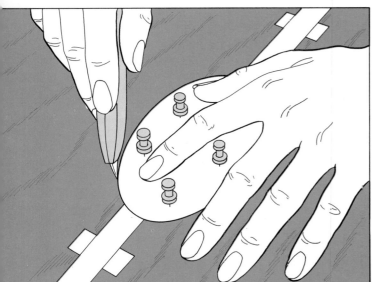

2 **Cutting the opening.** Slowly guide the sharp blade of a utility knife around the edge of the medallion, applying just enough pressure to score the underlying veneer. Caution: If you exert too much force on the knife, or work too quickly, the blade may slip and make an unwanted cut in the veneer; if that happens, tape the cut as if it were a seam. Make as many passes as necessary to cut all the way through the veneer. Then remove the pins, the medallion, and the cut section of veneer.

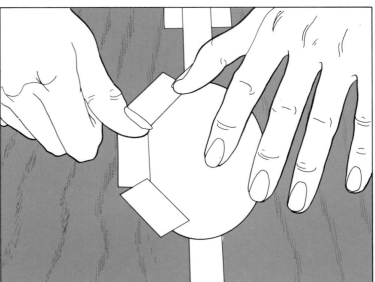

3 **Securing the medallion for bonding.** Place the medallion face up in the newly cut opening. Tape it in position, overlapping short strips of tape (*above*) so that they cover the entire joint with the surrounding veneer. Then turn the panel face down onto newspaper or brown wrapping paper, and brush contact cement onto the backs of the veneer and medallion and onto the surface of the tabletop. Following the directions on pages 92-94, Steps 11-16, bond the surfaces, trim the overhang with a chisel, and attach a band of veneer to the tabletop's vertical edge. ▶

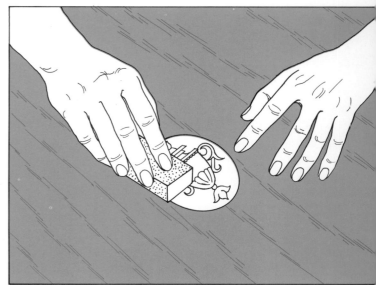

4 **Filling in a seam.** Remove the tape from the medallion and loosen the paper from its face by sanding it lightly, using fine (150-grit) sandpaper. If you find a slight gap between the veneer and the medallion, fill it in with wood plastic in the appropriate wood color, forcing the plastic into the crack with the blade of a screwdriver. Level the compound with the blade and scrape off any excess *(above)*, taking care not to scratch the veneer or inlay. Let the wood plastic dry for 30 minutes; then sand it smooth with very-fine (220-grit) sandpaper.

5 **Leveling the medallion.** Fit a sanding block with fine (150-grit) paper. Work with the grain to sand down the face of the medallion until it is flush with the surrounding veneer. Continue sanding over the whole surface of the veneer until the wood feels smooth. Then change to very-fine (220-grit) paper and sand lightly, to achieve a silky surface ready for finishing. Lastly, sand the table's edge and the arris *(page 94, Step 17)*.

Hide Glue: The Choice of Professionals

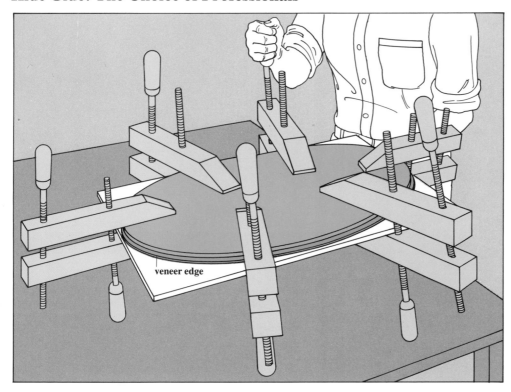

veneer edge

Hide glue, made from the hoofs, bones and hides of animals, is one of the oldest adhesives. And in spite of the development of contact cement, hide glue is still the choice among professional woodworkers because it bonds slowly, allowing adjustments in the positioning of veneer. However, it requires heavy, even pressure and many large clamps while drying.

The proper technique is to brush the hide glue onto the veneer and the furniture, and join the surfaces with the veneer overlapping the edges. Press out air bubbles with a hand roller before turning the veneer face down on a smooth surface and securing it with wood hand screws.

Fix the clamps at the ends and then at the sides of the piece; add others in between until the circumference is ringed with clamps 3 inches apart. Finally, pile heavy weights such as bricks on the center. Let the glue dry for 24 hours before trimming the veneer's edges with a chisel.

A formal border of inlaid strips

The key to employing ornamental inlay strips — like the diamond-patterned strips that elegantly define a border in the tray of the butler's table at left — is their positioning. Border strips are commonly placed about 1½ inches from the edge. Another factor in determining exact positioning of the strips is where on their decorative pattern the mitered corners will fall; the 45° ends of two strips should mate so the pattern is not broken but flows smoothly around the corner. Making a paper template of the surface to be veneered *(Step 1)* is essential to working out these problems.

Inlay strips are available in 3-foot lengths, ranging from ³⁄₁₆ to 1¼ inches in width. If you need a piece longer than 3 feet, place two strips in a line atop a cutting board with the end of one strip overlapping the end of the other by about 1 inch. Shift the strips until their patterns coincide, then cut through the overlap with a chisel. Tape the strips together to make one long strip.

If the strips are thicker than the veneer, you will later have to sand down the inlay *(opposite, Step 5)*.

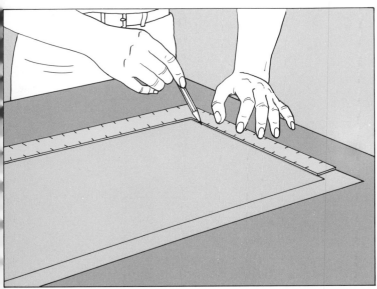

1 Making a paper template. Trace the outline of the object being veneered onto a sheet of paper. Trace a flat piece face down, but when dealing with a tray, as here, trace its bottom. Then measure the thickness of its vertical sides and — using a straightedge — draw new lines inside the traced ones to allow for the sides. Cut out the template and place it in the tray to check for fit. Because the tray may not be a perfect rectangle, mark one of its corners and the same corner of the template with masking tape, so you can match them later. Now draw lines 1½ inches from the edges of the template to indicate the placement of the strips' outside edges *(above)*. Use a carpenter's square: The inlay corners should be 90° angles whether the tray's corners are squared or not.

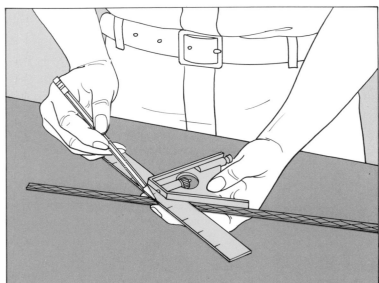

2 Positioning miters on the strips. Closely examine the pattern on two inlay strips to determine where the 45° cuts for a mitered corner should fall so the pattern will not be awkwardly broken. Once you think you have found a visually pleasing match, hold the 45° face of a combination square's head firmly against the edge of one inlay strip, and use the tool's blade as a guide to mark the angle across the strip *(above).* ▶

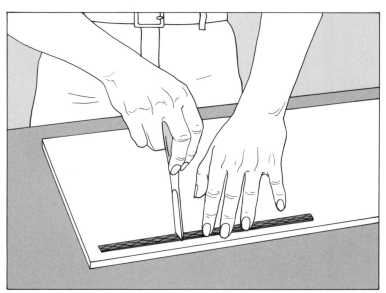

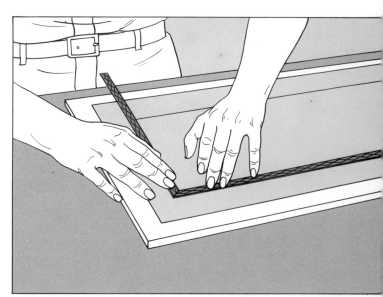

3 **Cutting the 45° angle.** Lay the strip on a cutting surface and position the blade of a sharp wood chisel — use one at least as wide as the strip — on the mark. While steadying the strip with your other hand, press the chisel down firmly to cut the inlay with one clean slice. Mark and cut a complementary miter on another strip and join them to see if they mate well. If you are not satisfied, experiment by cutting the miter in various locations on the design until you find a good combination.

4 **Fitting inlay strips together.** Lay the template on the cutting board. Align the outside edges of two strips with two adjacent pencil lines on the template, joining them at the mitered corner *(above)*. Examine where one strip crosses the opposite perpendicular pencil line: If a miter cut there would produce a different design match from the first corner, extend or shorten the strip for the fraction of an inch necessary to create an identical joint. Mark and cut that strip and its corner mate, then proceed to the next corner. When you have matched miters at corners all around, shift the strips as a unit until the outside margins are equal. Then pin the strips in place with veneer pins and trace those new positions onto the template. Remove the pins, strips and template.

7 **Cutting veneer for the margins.** With the template on a cutting board, measure one of its edges to find the length of the veneer section needed for that margin. Measure the width of the margin at two widely spaced points, in case the section needs to be wider at one end. (Precise measurements are necessary because the veneer has to fit into a tray; for a surface that is not enclosed you can let veneer overhang and trim it later.)

Using these dimensions and a straightedge, pencil the outline of the section onto a veneer sheet. Then cut the section out *(page 92)*, and place it in its position on the template. Measure and cut the other three margin sections, placing each on the template as you complete it. Making sure all four sections are precisely aligned with the appropriate template edges and lines, pin them in position — but leave their overlapping corners free of pins.

Now hold a straightedge firmly across a corner *(right)*, and guide a utility knife against it to cut from inside angle to outside angle, through both pieces of veneer. Cut the other mitered corners similarly.

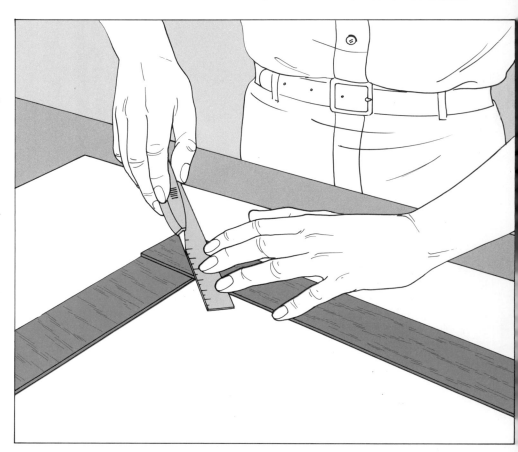

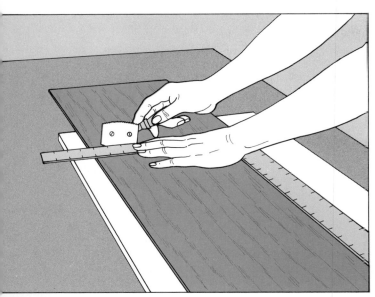

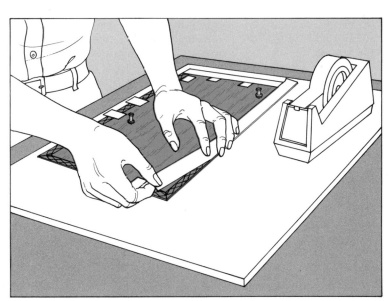

5 **Cutting the center veneer section.** Place the veneer panel smooth side up on the cutting board. For this tray, the center section of veneer can be cut from one sheet 12 inches wide, but for larger surfaces you may have to create a panel from two or more sheets *(pages 91-92, Steps 3-5).* Reassemble the inlay rectangle on the veneer, checking the corners with a carpenter's square, and pin it into place. Trace the inside edges of the rectangle onto the veneer, then remove the strips. Cut along the lines with a veneer saw, using a carpenter's square as a guide *(above).* Check the cutout section by placing it on the template with the strips. Trim it where necessary; if it is too small, cut out another piece. Sand any fuzzy edges with fine (150-grit) sandpaper.

6 **Taping the inlay strips to the center.** Pin the center section, face up, to the cutting board with veneer pins. Tightly butt the inlay strips against all four sides, carefully aligning them at the mitered corners. Tape each strip to the main body, first with short strips of tape across the joints every 5 inches or so, then with one long section of tape over each seam. Remove the pins and turn the panel over to make sure each joint is tight. If there are gaps, remove the tape and fit the pieces together again.

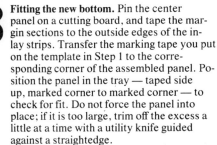

8 **Fitting the new bottom.** Pin the center panel on a cutting board, and tape the margin sections to the outside edges of the inlay strips. Transfer the marking tape you put on the template in Step 1 to the corresponding corner of the assembled panel. Position the panel in the tray — taped side up, marked corner to marked corner — to check for fit. Do not force the panel into place; if it is too large, trim off the excess a little at a time with a utility knife guided against a straightedge.

When the panel fits, remove it and cover the tray's inner sides with masking tape to protect them from adhesive. Then apply contact cement to the tray and the veneer *(pages 92-93, Steps 11-12).* Remove the masking tape from the tray so the panel will fit easily. Bond the panel to the tray *(page 93, Step 13),* and sand down the inlay strips *(page 102, Step 5).* Sand and finish the veneer *(page 94, Step 17).*

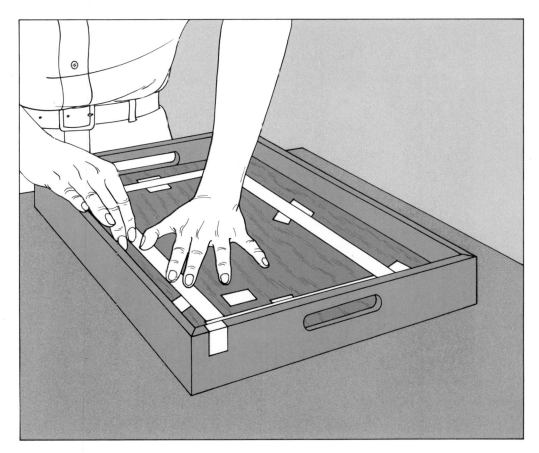

A centerpiece of tooled leather

ew furniture-finishing materials elicit such admiration as leather tooled with a pattern of gold. Inlaid on the top of a chest, a table or a desk like the one below, leather conveys a sense of worth and heritage both to the eye and to the fingertips that inevitably explore its texture.

Creating a leather centerpiece for a desk top that has squared edges requires only that you build up a border of veneer *(page 113)* to form a recess for the inlay. But if the top has rounded or molded edges to which veneer cannot be attached easily in the home workshop, you will need to make a whole new top.

The desk below was given a new top built of plywood with a hardwood border surrounding the inlay (the hardwood here is walnut, to match the old desk). In order to make the top look the age of the rest of the desk, the border was distressed, by the methods described on pages 32-33, before the leather was applied. The steps that follow show how to construct the hardwood-bordered top, and how to apply and tool the leather.

In building a top, the key consideration is to have the border $\frac{1}{32}$ to $\frac{1}{16}$ inch higher

than the central opening, so that the inlaid leather will be just about flush with the surrounding wood. This can be achieved by using $\frac{3}{4}$-inch-thick plywood for the center and framing it with hardwood that is nominally 1 inch thick. Since the actual thickness of nominal 1-inch hardwood that has been planed smooth on both its wide surfaces is about $\frac{13}{16}$ of an inch, the border will be approximately $\frac{1}{16}$ inch higher than the plywood.

Because the pieces need perfectly squared edges to fit together in butt joints, it is wise to have the lumberyard cut the wood to size. Explain to the dealer how you plan to use the wood, so the importance of accurate cuts will be clear.

The dimensions of the pieces depend on the desk top you are replacing. Measure the old top and ask the dealer to cut a rectangular sheet of plywood 4 inches smaller in both length and width. Birch plywood is a good choice, because it will provide a smooth underlay for the leather at an economical price; the surfaces of such construction plywood as fir are too rough for the job.

Specify that the hardwood for the border be free of knots and blemishes and be

surfaced — planed smooth — on all four sides. The border will have a width of 2 inches. Hardwood is not sold in standard widths, so the dealer will cut the strips from a wider board. Make it clear that the wood must be 2 inches wide after the edges have been planed smooth. The two hardwood pieces that will stretch along the front and back of the desk top should be 4 inches longer than the plywood. The two endpieces should be exactly as long as the plywood is wide.

Obtaining the leather may be somewhat more difficult than buying the wood, but not much. Merchants who sell leather for crafts and upholstery can be found in even medium-sized towns. Some mail-order firms offer suitable leather, too.

For a desk top about the size of this one — 46 by 24 inches — you will probably have to buy a portion of cowhide known as a side (half a complete hide), or at the least half a side. Take to the dealer a template of the area to be inlaid *(Step 9)*, to make sure you buy a piece that is large enough. Tell the dealer what you want the leather for and ask for a pre-dyed, smooth-grained hide weighing 1½ to 2 ounces per square foot. Leather of

his weight is strong and yet thin enough to be used as an inlay.

The leather dealer can also supply a potassium lactate preservative to prevent the leather from absorbing decay-causing acid *(Step 9)*. Additionally, the dealer will have leather dressing — a mixture of lanolin and neat's-foot oil — to coat the hide's face and help keep it moist and supple.

The treated leather is best glued in place with a paste made from wheat starch or rice starch (similar to, but not the same as, common wallpaper paste, which contains additives). The starch can be bought from bookbinding suppliers and some wallpaper shops; ask for unmodified wheat starch.

After the leather is installed and treated, it is ready for tooling. The 23-karat gold used for imprinting the design comes as a thin film bonded to a tape of clear polyester. The tape is sold in 1-inch-wide rolls by bookbinding suppliers and some mail-order houses. Normally it is available only in rolls 200 feet long, many times as much as needed for an inlay of this size; however, the cost is not prohibitive. Imitation gold foil can be had for 1/10 the price, but it tarnishes quickly.

The best imprinting tools for home use are brass stamps, hand-cut for sharp impressions and available from bookbinding suppliers. Less expensive chrome-plated stamps from leather-goods stores will also serve. To transfer the gold to the inlay, the stamp is heated and then pressed onto the tape by hand *(Steps 16 and 17)*; a stamp hit by a mallet might cut the leather. Attaining the correct temperature for the stamp is essential. If the stamp is too hot, the gold on the leather will look burnt. If it is not hot enough, it will not imprint the whole pattern.

Some other tools needed are a narrow paint roller and paint-roller tray for applying the adhesive, and a bone folder — a smooth, rounded bone or plastic oblong that bookbinders use for pressing down leather after pasting it. Lacking a bone folder, you can substitute a comb with a smooth, rounded back.

Replacing a deteriorated leather inlay on an existing furniture top is, of course, much simpler. Begin by using a chisel or putty knife to scrape up one corner of the old leather so you can dissolve the underlying adhesive. Usually the adhesive will be a wheat or rice paste dried to a hard,

whitish substance that will soften when moistened repeatedly with water from a spray bottle. If the adhesive is instead rubbery and amber-colored, it is contact cement and can be loosened by brushing on a nonflammable adhesive solvent.

Free one end of the inlay, roll the loosened leather onto a dowel or broomstick and pull up the leather inch by inch as you dissolve the adhesive. When the inlay has been removed, scrape the recess clean, fill any dents with wood putty and sand the area smooth. Then prepare, apply and tool the new leather inlay *(Steps 9-17)*.

Materials List	
Wood	1 " hardwood, 2 " wide, cut into 4 strips to fit the desk top ¾ " plywood, cut to fit the desk top 1 box ⅜ " hardwood dowel plugs
Leather	1 piece smooth-grained, predyed leather for desk-top inlay
Screws	12 No. 10 flat-head wood screws, 2½ " long
Gold	1 roll 23-karat gold foil

1 **Removing the old desk top.** Measure and note the overhang of the desk top. Some tops overhang on all sides; others are flush with the desk at the back. You will need the information later, when you position the new top. Remove the drawers and open any doors to locate the screws holding the top in place. In this case, screws securing the top are driven up through glue blocks *(inset)* at each end and along the front and back of the desk; sometimes screws are driven at an angle up through the sides of the desk into the top. Remove the screws with a screwdriver *(above)*. If the top is also glued in place, break the glue bonds by inserting a chisel into each seam from inside the desk and tapping with a hammer until all sides are loose. Remove the top.

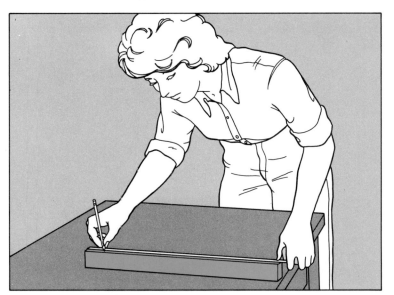

2 **Marking screw holes on a border piece.** Place one of the short hardwood boards — cut to form one end of the border — on edge on a worktable. Measure for and draw a lengthwise line along the center of the top edge. Then make cross marks on this line 2 inches from each end and in the middle. Mark the other short board similarly. The marks indicate the positions of screws that will hold the boards to the ends of the plywood. ▶

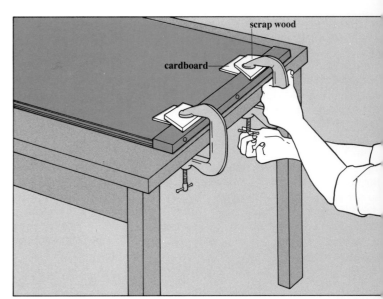

3 **Drilling the screw holes.** To bore the wide holes in which screwheads will be recessed and concealed by plugs, fit a power drill with a ⅜-inch twist bit. Wrap masking tape around the bit ¾ inch from the tip, so you will know when the hole is ¾ inch deep. Holding one of the short hardwood boards on edge on a piece of scrap wood *(above)*, drill straight down at the marked screw positions, stopping when the tape on the bit reaches the surface of the wood. After drilling at all the marked places on both short boards, fit the drill with a ¼-inch twist bit, center the bit in each of the wide holes and drill the rest of the way through the boards to make holes for the screw shanks *(inset)*. Use sandpaper to remove any splinters created when the bit tip emerges from the wood.

4 **Aligning the end boards with the plywood center.** On a level work surface, butt long edges of the short hardwood boards — with the wide holes to the outside — against the ends of the plywood. Align the ends of the boards with the edges of the plywood. Then position scraps of cardboard on the plywood next to the boards to form level surfaces for C clamps that will hold the pieces together. Fasten the clamps over the seams, protecting the hardwood from the clamp jaws with scrap wood.

6 **Fastening the pieces together.** Run a line of yellow carpenter's glue along the plywood ends and the inside edges of the hardwood boards. Reposition the hardwood boards against the plywood and fasten them with 2½-inch No. 10 flathead wood screws. Wipe away any excess glue with a damp cloth.

Now mark screw-hole positions on the two long hardwood boards: Draw a lengthwise line along the center of one long edge of each board and make cross marks on that line 1 inch from each end and at the midpoint. In this case the screws near the ends will fasten the long boards to the butting ends of the shorter boards, not to the plywood. Drill the holes and fix the boards to the already-assembled pieces of the desk top by following the procedures described in Steps 3 through 5.

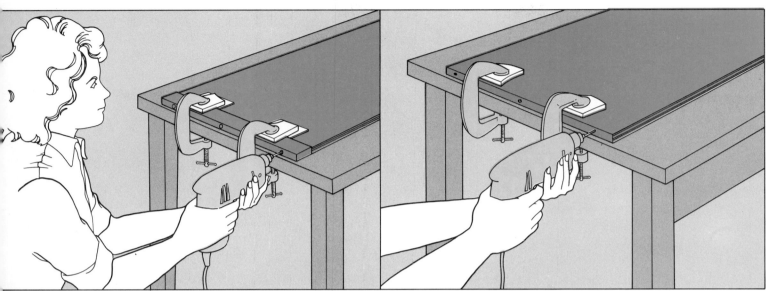

5 **Drilling pilot holes in the plywood.** To mark the positions for pilot holes in the edge of the plywood, slip the ¼-inch bit through each of the screw holes in turn, and switch the drill on and off quickly while the bit tip is against the plywood *(above, left)*. Then remove the clamps and the hardwood boards, and clamp only the plywood to the table. Fit the

drill with a ⅛-inch bit. Wrap the bit with masking tape 1¼ inches from the tip. Now drill straight into the plywood edge *(above, right)* at each position that was marked by the spinning ¼-inch bit; stop when the tape on the bit reaches the wood.

7 **Inserting the dowel plugs.** Pour a small amount of carpenter's glue into a shallow dish and dip a ⅜-inch hardwood dowel plug into the glue. Place the plug into a screw hole and with a wooden mallet gently tap the dowel into the hole until it is flush with the surface of the surrounding wood. If you are tapping with a hammer instead of a mallet, place a wood scrap over the dowel to avoid damaging the hardwood. Plug the other screw holes in the same manner and let the glue dry for one hour. Then, if necessary, distress the hardwood *(pages 32-33)* to make it match the base of the desk. Finally, sand and finish the hardwood.

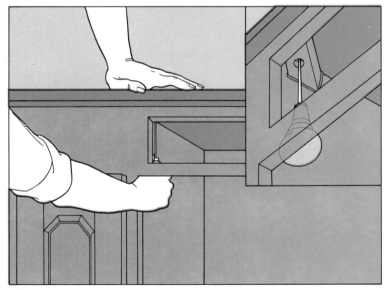

8 **Mounting the new top.** Position the new top on the desk just as the old top was positioned *(Step 1)*. Push an awl up through the glue-block holes to mark screw locations on the bottom of the new top *(above and in-set)*. If the old top was fastened with screws angled up through the sides, push the awl through these holes. Now turn the top upside down. Fit a drill with a ⅛-inch bit, and mark the bit with masking tape ½ inch from the tip. Drill pilot holes at the awl marks, stopping when the tape reaches the wood. If the old top was fastened by angled screws, approximate the angles while drilling. Finally, fix the new top in place with wood screws the same size as those removed from the old top. ▶

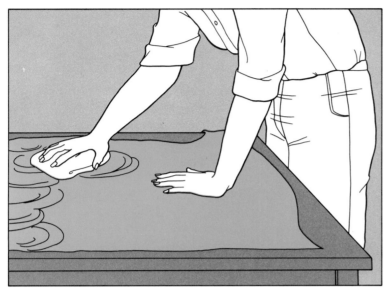

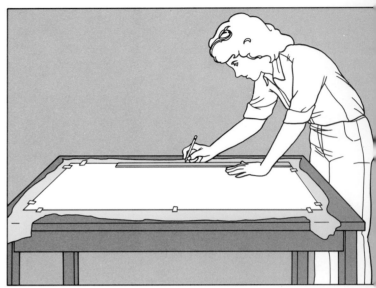

9 **Buying and treating the leather.** To make a template for the leather, cover the recess of the desk top with a large sheet of paper, and mark the outline of the recess with a pencil. Then draw new lines ¼ inch outside the ones you just marked. Cut the template along the outside lines, and check to make sure it is slightly larger than the recess. Take the template to the leather supplier and select an unmarred piece of leather large enough to cover it. If you wish, apply a thin coat of potassium lactate to the leather with a soft cloth, rubbing the preservative in with a circular motion *(above)*. The next day, apply leather dressing, a mixture of lanolin and neat's-foot oil. Let the leather dry for three days before wiping off the excess.

10 **Tracing the template onto the leather.** Place the leather on the table with the flesh side — the fuzzy underside — upward, and tape the template to it with short strips of masking tape. Using a soft lead pencil guided by a wooden straightedge (metal might discolor the leather), transfer the template's outline onto the leather. Then cut the leather along the pencil lines with sharp scissors.

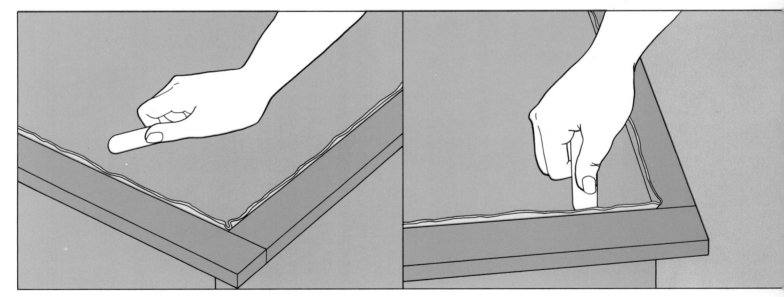

13 **Eliminating air bubbles.** Immediately after positioning the leather in the recess, press its surface with a bone folder, or the back of a comb, to squeeze out air bubbles. Hold the folder on one long edge *(above, left)* and push it across the surface while exerting downward pressure. After pressing the whole inlay — a process that will stretch the leather slightly — use an end of the folder *(above, right)* to crease the overlapping leather against the border.

11 **Applying the adhesive.** For a top of this size — 46 by 24 inches — mix 1 cup of wheat or rice starch with 4 cups of water, stirring steadily until you obtain a smooth consistency. If the mixture gets lumpy, strain it by pressing it through a coarse sieve with a wooden spoon. Pour the paste into a paint-roller tray and thoroughly moisten a narrow paint roller in the adhesive. Roll it evenly onto the recessed surface of the desk top, making sure not to skimp on adhesive along the edges. Let the adhesive set for about 15 minutes, until it feels slightly tacky.

12 **Positioning the leather in the recess.** Lay the leather out on a table with the grain side — the smooth side — up, and roll it loosely back on itself. Position one corner of the leather in a corner of the recess and smooth it down with your hand *(above)*. Unroll the leather, pressing it down onto the adhesive as you go. Smooth it first toward one corner that is adjacent to where you started, then to the other adjacent corner, finally toward the diagonally placed corner. Make sure the leather extends to all edges of the recess; it will lap up over two of the edges. Use a damp cloth to wipe away any glue that squeezes out along the edges.

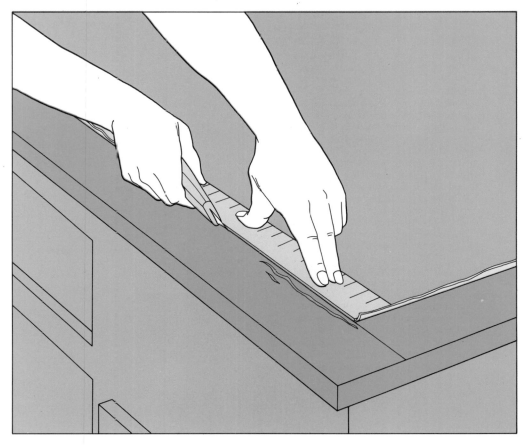

14 **Trimming off the excess leather.** As soon as you have worked out air bubbles with the bone folder, start trimming the excess leather from the edges; do it before the adhesive dries completely so you can still stretch the leather with the folder if you trim off a little too much. Use a sharp utility knife held against a wooden straightedge. Hold the knife handle angled slightly away from the inlay surface so the blade does not expose a white edge of the leather as it slices. If you find that an edge of the leather is not firmly stuck down, pull it up far enough to spread more paste underneath, then press it back into place. When you have trimmed all the edges, press them again with the end of the folder. Then let the adhesive dry overnight. ▶

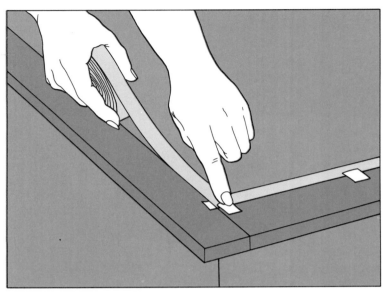

15 **Positioning the gold.** Unroll a strip of gold foil and lay it shiny side up (the duller side bears the gold) on the leather along one edge of the inlay, against the wood trim. Use scissors to cut the strip to the length of the edge. Tape the foil to the wood at each end and several places in between with bits of masking tape, making sure the tape does not obscure any part of the foil that you will use for tooling. Tape foil along the other three edges of the leather in the same way, overlapping the corners. You can use the foil's inner edge as a guideline for the stamping tool, but if you want your design closer to the edge of the leather, draw guidelines on the foil with a fine-point felt-tipped pen and a wood straightedge.

16 **Heating the stamp.** Place the pattern end of the tooling stamp on an electric or gas burner, or in a liquid-fuel flame, for about two minutes. Then lightly touch the heated surface of the stamp with a wet sponge; if you hear a hissing sound, the stamp is hot enough for use. Make sure it is not too hot by testing it on gold foil on a scrap piece of leather; if the imprinted gold looks burnt, cool the stamp by touching it against the sponge again. Test it once more.

17 **Tooling the leather.** The first imprint must turn the corner, so position the stamp over the intersection of two guidelines and rotate it to make the design fall at a 45° angle to both lines. Holding the handle perpendicular to the surface, push down with both hands, exerting steady pressure. Then rock the stamp to ensure that the edges of the design are imprinted. Now lift the stamp and move it into position for the next imprint, this time aligning it squarely with the guideline.

Monitor the thickness of the gold transferred to the leather by occasionally lifting the edge of the foil. As soon as the gold in the impression begins to appear thin, reheat the stamp. When the distance to the next corner leaves about enough space for six more impressions, stamp in that corner design and space the intervening stamps evenly *(right)*, so you will not have a large gap just before the corner. Continue all the way around the inlay. The gold is now permanently affixed.

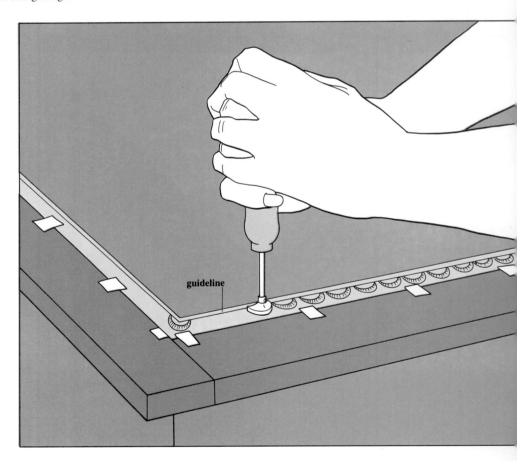

guideline

A Veneer Frame for Leather

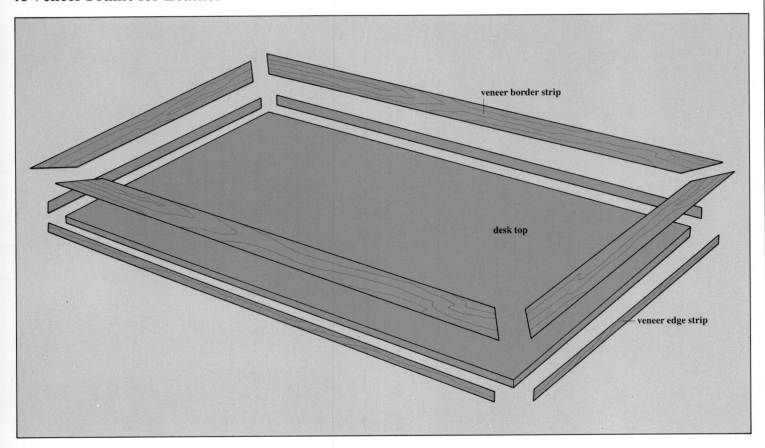

veneer border strip

desk top

veneer edge strip

Another way to create a new, leather-inlaid desk top — or to convert an old desk top so a leather inlay can be added to it — is by using veneer. This method involves less carpentry than the method described on the preceding pages.

For a new top, as the drawing above shows, four 2-inch-wide strips of veneer, with mitered corners, are fixed to a base of plywood or particleboard as a border for the inlay. The edges are then covered with narrower veneer strips. The same veneer arrangement can form an inlay border on an old desk top, if the top's edges are squared, rather than beveled or rounded.

If you are making a new top, buy ¾-inch plywood or particleboard with smooth surfaces. Have it cut to the dimensions of the top you are replacing. The edges of plywood or particleboard must be filled with wood plastic and then sanded smooth with a sanding block before veneer can be attached.

Select veneer that matches the wood of the desk. The veneer must be at least as thick as the leather inlay so the white edge of the leather will not show. Veneer ⅟₃₂ or ⅟₂₈ inch thick probably will do the job. If the leather is thicker than the veneer, you can glue two layers of veneer together (*page 118, Step 4*) before cutting them to size.

The basic tools and methods for cutting pieces of veneer, assembling them into units and fixing them in place with contact cement are described on pages 90-94. For this project, where the grain must run lengthwise in every piece, buy sheets of veneer that are at least as long as the pieces you need. That way you will not have to make any unsightly across-the-grain splices.

For the front and back of the border, cut two 2-inch-wide strips of veneer to the exact length of the desk top. Cut the endpieces as long as the top is wide. Overlap the ends of the perpendicular pieces to cut the 45° angles for

the mitered corners (*page 104, Step 7*). Tape the veneer pieces together, making sure the mitered joints are snug. Then attach the border to the desk top with contact cement, using a slip sheet to position it (*page 93, Step 12*). Trim away any overhang with a chisel.

The veneer strips that will cover the edges of the desk top should be ¼ inch wider than the edge — thus, 1 inch wide if the new top is ¾ inch thick. And each strip should be ½ inch longer than the edge to which it will be affixed. Attach the endpieces first, aligning them with the surface of the veneer border so the ¼-inch margin hangs below the desk-top edge. The strip should extend ¼ inch beyond the desk-top corners. After trimming the end strips with a chisel, attach and trim the front and back strips similarly. Then sand the arrises of all corners and edges, and finish the veneer strips as desired. You are now ready to apply and tool the leather (*pages 110-112, Steps 9-17*).

Face-lifts for damaged veneer

Mending old veneer is cosmetic surgery that requires only patience and a steady hand to achieve remarkable results. Most damaged veneer can be renewed by four basic repairs: regluing loose or broken pieces of old veneer, filling tiny cracks and chips, regluing bubbled veneer, and replacing missing pieces of veneer. The 18th Century chest shown here both before *(inset)* and after repair illustrates how such delicate surgery, followed by chemical stripping *(pages 34-35)* and a new finish, can heal even extensive ravages, whether in small elements or large sheets of veneer. Veneering furniture from scratch *(pages 90-94)* is required only if the old veneer is so shredded that it can be scraped from its base.

Before repairing flawed veneer, you must diagnose and cure the underlying cause of the damage, which otherwise may recur. Loose or missing pieces of veneer signal a weak glue bond between the veneer and base. This can be caused by direct sunlight or by heat from a radiator or forced-air vent. Or it may result from excessive moisture that has seeped into the glue joints, perhaps through a cracked, and thus permeable, finish.

Bubbles or cracks suggest that the veneer and base expand and contract at different rates in response to changing humidity. This is particularly a problem if the base is solid lumber rather than a more stable material such as plywood or particleboard.

In well-crafted solid furniture, veneer covers the base's bottom as well as its top, to balance moisture retention. Occasionally bubbles or cracks are caused by an irredeemably bad design: If the ve-

neer's grain is parallel to that of the base or if the base consists of many small boards that have expanded or contracted, damaged veneer cannot be repaired satisfactorily.

The essential techniques for veneer repairs are quite similar to those for applying new veneer: removing the furniture's doors, drawers and hardware; filling holes and dents in the base; sanding the surface smooth and wiping away every trace of dust; and gluing down the veneer's rough side, leaving the smooth side for the finished surface. However, repairing veneer also involves a few specialized tricks and tools.

To reach under loose or bubbled veneer you will need two palette knives whose blunt, supple blades can lift fragile veneer without breaking it. A sloyd knife *(Step 3),* a sturdy woodworking tool that

as a sharp, pointed blade about 3¼ inches long, is invaluable for scraping old glue from the base and the veneer; the best substitute would be a knife with a blade so rigid that it has no flex. If the old veneer is fastened by contact cement, a rubbery-looking adhesive used on recently made furniture, you will need to remove it with nonflammable adhesive solvent, which can be safely used only in a well-ventilated room. Protect the area around the repair with masking tape before using the solvent to clean the base and the old veneer *(Step 3)*.

Regardless of the veneer's old adhesive, repaired veneer should be fastened with hide glue *(page 102)*. For repair work it is considerably more forgiving than the contact cement used for whole sheets of veneer, because it allows adjustments after application.

Glue alone can repair loose or bubbled veneer, but to replace a missing piece you will have to select a new veneer that matches the surrounding wood's grain and figuring. You also may need to build up the replacement piece's thickness. Modern veneers typically are ¹⁄₂₈ to ¹⁄₆₀ inch thick, while old ones vary considerably and sometimes reach ⅛ inch in thickness. To match the old thickness you can glue together two to four layers of veneer *(page 118, Step 4)*, making a thick sandwich that will later be sanded flush with the surrounding surface.

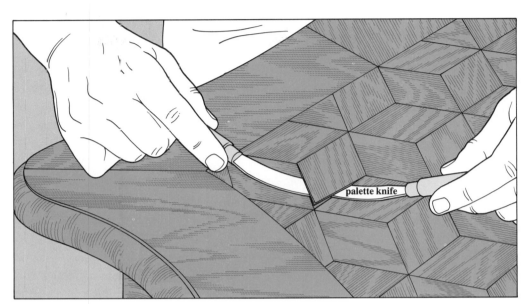

1 **Separating the loose piece.** Slip a palette knife under the loose piece of veneer and gently raise the flap of veneer about ¼ inch. To completely separate the loose veneer from the base, slide another palette knife under the loose piece, then gently work it sideways and in and out, stopping when the blade reaches solidly glued areas. Save the loose piece if it breaks off, as often happens; the jagged fracture line will be virtually invisible when the repair is completed.

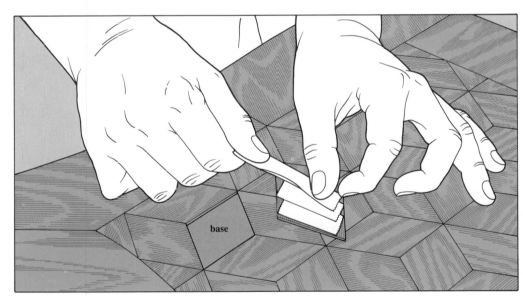

2 **Reinforcing the loose veneer.** Whether the loosened piece remains attached or snaps off, as here, check its appearance. If the piece looks splintery, feels brittle or resists bending — a common problem with long-grained woods such as oak, teak and chestnut — cover the piece with overlapping strips of ½-inch masking tape placed parallel to the grain. ▶

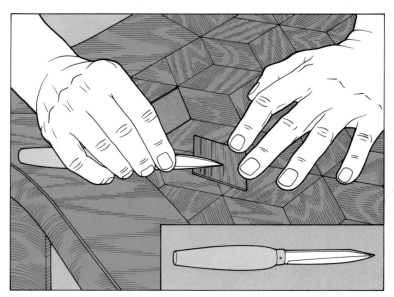

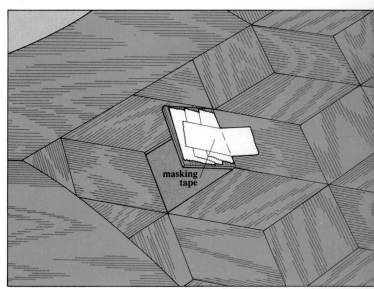

3 **Removing old glue.** If the loosened piece remains attached to the furniture, support its upper side with one hand; if it has broken off, place it upside down. If the veneer and base are covered with hard, brittle traces of old hide glue, scrape along the veneer's grain with a sharp sloyd knife *(inset)* until you expose bare wood, devoid of all traces of glue. If you see the gummy traces of contact cement, put masking tape on adjacent veneer to isolate it, then thoroughly wipe the veneer's underside with a cotton swab soaked in a nonflammable adhesive solvent; wait about 20 minutes and scrape away the resulting residue with a palette knife. Using whichever method is appropriate, scrape away any glue on the veneer's edges and the base. Remove all dust with a dry paintbrush.

4 **Aligning the piece.** If the loose veneer has broken off, set the piece in its original position. Run a hingelike strip of masking tape across the piece and onto one adjoining surface. Then use a palette knife *(Step 1)* to pivot the piece on this hinge until its bottom faces up.

Mending a Tiny Flaw

All too often, veneered furniture is marred by hairline cracks and tiny chips. Flaws more than ¼ inch across can be filled with the original piece of veneer *(Steps 3-6, above)*, if it can be found, or with a custom-fitted new piece *(pages 118-119)*. But smaller faults must be subtly patched with a cosmetic filler.

Finished furniture can be patched with melted shellac or lacquer *(page 121)*, both of which are available in sticks whose colors match most woods. But on furniture that is slated for stripping and refinishing, wood plastic *(right)* or a similar putty-like patching compound provides better results. Unlike shellac and lacquer, such compounds blend seamlessly into a surface: Their initial color, chosen to match that of the bare wood, will absorb stains and finishes just as the surrounding veneer does.

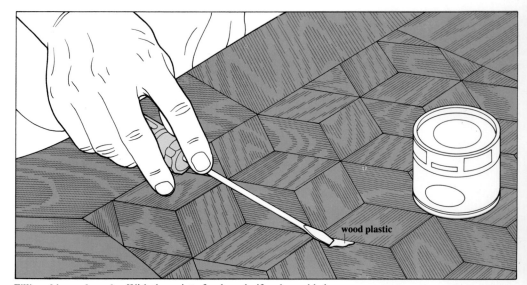

Filling chips and cracks. With the point of a sharp knife, clean old glue from each recess until you reach bare wood *(Step 3, above)*, using a nonflammable adhesive solvent if you discover traces of contact cement. When the recess is clean and dry, dab wood plastic onto the tip of a screwdriver and press it into the recess, slightly overfilling the void to allow for shrinkage. Smooth the patch with the screwdriver and let it dry for 30 minutes; then sand the patch flush with the veneer.

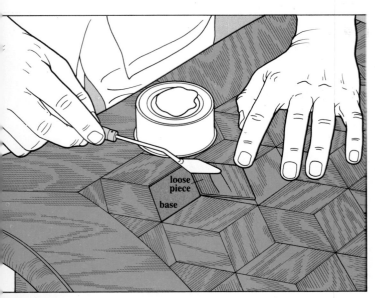

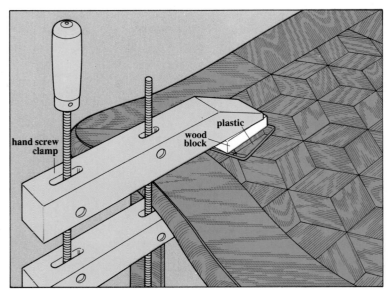

5 **Gluing the pieces.** Turn an empty tin can upside down and put a table-spoon or so of hide glue on its bottom. Using a palette knife as you would a spatula, spread a thin, even layer of glue on the veneer piece's bottom and edges. Spread glue on the base in the same way, if possible, working it under the adjoining veneer with the palette knife's tip. Press the hinged piece of veneer against the base with your fingers, then use the palette knife to gently scrape away excess glue as it wells up around the piece's edges. To remove the last bits of glue, wipe the edges with a paper towel dampened in warm water.

6 **Clamping the piece.** Cut a piece of stiff sheet plastic or wax paper that will overlap the reglued piece of veneer by about ½ inch on each side, and place it on the veneer. Put a roughly matching block of plywood or 1-inch lumber on the plastic or the wax paper. Apply about 40 pounds of pressure to the block for 24 hours: Use a hand screw (box, page 102) if the repair is near a clampable edge; use a stack of gym weights, bricks or books if the repair cannot be clamped.

Flattening a Bubble

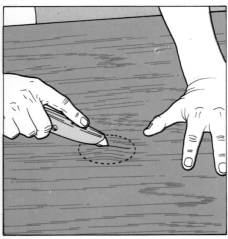

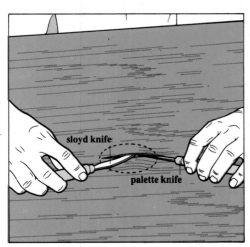

1 **Cutting the bubble.** Using a razor-sharp utility knife, cut across the entire bubble parallel to the grain, slicing clear through the veneer. If the bubble is more than 2½ inches wide across the grain, make additional parallel cuts every 1½ inches. With your hands, press flat the bubble's sliced edges. If they overlap, lift the top edge and scrape away tiny slivers, holding the knife perpendicular to the edge, until the edges butt together neatly.

2 **Removing the old glue.** Lift each of the bubble's sliced edges with a palette knife. Scrape away old glue from the base and veneer inside the bubble with a sloyd knife, holding the blade nearly parallel to the base. If the knife blade reveals gummy contact cement, clear the bubble with non-flammable adhesive solvent (Step 3, above left). While still holding up the edge, blow out the old glue from inside and sweep away the residue with a brush.

3 **Regluing the veneer.** Place about a tablespoon of hide glue on a tin can. With a palette knife spread a thin layer of glue inside the bubble on both the veneer and the base, working glue into the bubble's farthest recesses. Working parallel to the grain, traverse the bubble repeatedly with a hand roller, bearing down hard to squeeze excess glue out of the slit. Wipe glue from the slit with a damp paper towel, and clamp the glued area (Step 6, above).

Replacing a Missing Piece

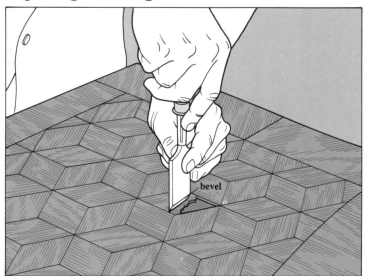

1 **Straightening difficult edges.** If the veneered edges around a missing piece are not perfectly straight, plan a chisel cut that runs roughly parallel to the veneer's grain about ¼ inch behind each jagged edge; avoid cross-grained cuts, which leave noticeable lines around the new piece. Using a wood chisel narrower than the cut, set the blade behind one end of the edge, its bevel facing the exposed base, and push the blade straight down through the veneer. Extend the cut to the edge's other end in the same way. Scrape away glue and debris from the base *(page 116, Step 3)*, then brush away the dust with a brush.

2 **Making a paper pattern.** Hold a small sheet of paper over the recess left by the missing piece, and with your index finger rub the paper atop each of the surrounding veneer's edges. With scissors cut the paper just outside the impressed lines. Test the resulting pattern in place of the missing piece; if necessary, trim the pattern until each side extends barely ⅟₃₂ inch beyond the old veneer's edges.

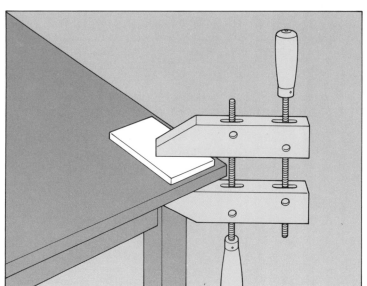

4 **Matching the old thickness.** Cut a tiny scrap of veneer and place it in the recess. If the scrap is thinner than the surrounding veneer, use a veneer saw *(page 92)* to cut a rectangular piece that includes the penciled outline marked in Step 3, and also cut enough matching rectangles to exceed the old veneer's thickness. Apply hide glue to each piece in turn and stack the pieces with their grain running parallel. Clamp the rectangles under a scrap of plywood; use a single hand screw for pieces less than 3 inches square, one hand screw or C clamp on each side for larger pieces. Let the glue set for 24 hours.

5 **Cutting a long edge.** To make cuts more than 2 inches long, first put the veneer sheet or stacked rectangles of veneer on a plywood scrap. Hold a metal ruler or a carpenter's square just outside the pencil line, set the bottom of a veneer saw vertically against the metal straightedge and repeatedly draw the saw toward you until it cuts through the veneer.

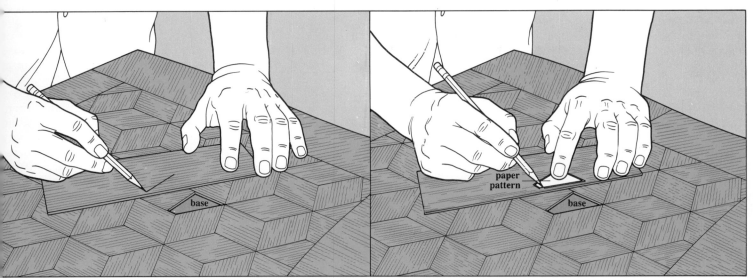

3 **Choosing the new piece.** To select a replacement piece for veneer such as that shown here, align a veneer sheet's grain with that needed for the new piece, and lay the sheet beside the exposed base, with the veneer's smooth side up *(page 91, Step 2)*. Slowly slide the sheet by the base until you find a new section whose color, grain and figure approximate those of the pieces that will surround it. To duplicate the look of finished veneer, moisten a spot within this new section with water

and compare its color to the surroundings. When you settle on a matching section, pencil a rough outline of the new piece on it *(above, left)*. Then put the paper pattern from Step 2 inside the outline, make sure the grain is aligned correctly and trace around the pattern *(above)*.

To find a replacement piece that will fit into a large sheet of veneer, use a cardboard viewer *(page 98, Step 4)* to match the appearances of the new veneer and the old veneer.

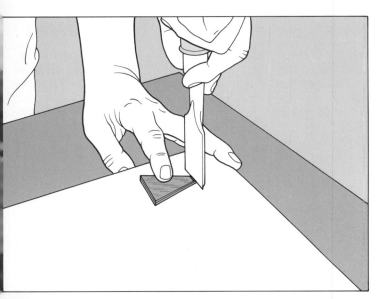

6 **Cutting a short edge.** On edges that are less than 2 inches long, a wood chisel cuts much faster than a saw: Place the veneer on the plywood scrap, and set the blade of a 2-inch chisel on the pencil line, with its beveled side facing away from the new piece. Hold the chisel vertically and push it straight down through the veneer.

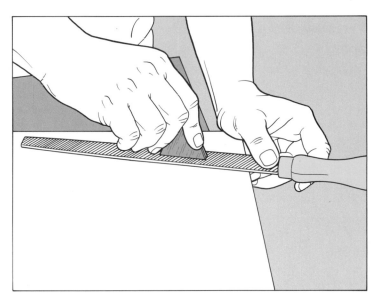

7 **Fitting the new piece.** Test the new veneer in its recess, and mark the edges that overlap the surrounding veneer. To trim these edges hold a single-cut mill file — a flat file with one set of parallel grooves — on a worktable. Slide each marked edge of the veneer piece back and forth along the file, keeping the veneer's face perpendicular to the file. Test the piece again after every one or two strokes. When the new piece fits perfectly, glue down the rough side *(page 117, Steps 5-6)* and sand the top side flush with the surrounding surface, using a sanding block fitted with fine (150-grit) paper.

Repairing damaged woods

All furniture inevitably suffers some kind of damage to the surface. It gets cracked, scratched, dented, burned, stained by water, parched by the sun. Before you refinish a piece, you should attempt repairs. In some cases, the damage can be erased completely; it always can be rendered less conspicuous.

Hairline cracks in shellac or lacquer finish, caused by the desiccating effect of sunlight, can be rubbed out with paste wax and 4/0 steel wool. If the cracks are larger than hairlines, wipe them with a liquid refinisher, available at hardware stores. The liquid refinisher should dissolve the finish and cause it to seep into the cracks, filling them up. If the result is unsatisfactory, strip the piece (*pages 34-35*) and refinish it.

Wax finishes are susceptible to another atmospheric problem — high humidity, which gives them an unattractive, cloudy look. The clouding can be eliminated completely by wiping the surface with a cloth dipped in mineral spirits.

A wood surface that has been dented can often be restored by steaming out the indentation with an iron (*below, left*). Like a sponge, the compressed wood fibers will absorb the steam and swell up to the surface.

Burn marks present a more serious challenge. First, rub or scrape away the charred wood fibers (*below, center*); then fill the resulting hole. Wax pencils, commonly used to cover up tiny nicks and scratches, offer a temporary solution. But wax is soft, comes in only a few wood colors and accepts stain poorly.

Wood putty is far more effective and just as easy to apply. It comes in all common wood colors and can be sanded, stained and finished like real wood. You can use any stain on wood putty, but powders called padding stains, applied over a padding finish (*page 122*), are specifically made for such spot repairs.

For the best results with scratches, dents and holes, use a lacquer or shellac stick, the filler used by professionals. It can be purchased through furniture-refinishing suppliers — along with a compound for leveling its surface and a thick felt block for applying the compound. The sticks come in typical stain colors, so after applying a shellac-stick patch (*opposite*), you do not need to restain. Select a color slightly darker than the color of your wood. The darker color will disguise the patch and make it look like a natural feature of the wood's graining.

Water marks pose the toughest problems. The white water rings that form when a wet glass sits too long on a shellac or lacquer surface can be rubbed away with rottenstone or pumice powders, mild abrasives sold at hardware stores. Try rottenstone first: It is less likely to mar the finish surrounding the damage.

Dark water stains, typically the result of a flowerpot dripping for weeks onto a coffee table, are a sign of deeper trouble: The water has eaten through the finish into the wood itself. The only solution is to strip off the finish and bleach the wood (*page 27*). Often you must bleach the entire surface of the piece to achieve uniform color. Only then can the wood be restained and refinished to its original depth and hue.

Steaming Out a Small Dent

With stripper, a soft cloth and steel wool, remove the finish (*pages 34-35*) around the dent. Dampen a small cotton cloth with water, fold it and place it on the dent. Invert a metal bottle cap over it. Then press the tip of a hot iron into the cap (*below*). Steam the dent for five minutes or until the wood fibers rise flush with the surface. Let the fibers dry, then sand and refinish the area.

bottle cap

Effacing a Burn Mark

Rub the burn mark with 4/0 steel wool. If this fails to obliterate the mark, sprinkle on a thin layer of fine pumice and use a dampened cloth to rub the pumice into the charred wood. If the mark still persists, scrape out the charred wood with the blade of a knife (*below*). Then fill the resulting hole with a shellac-stick (*opposite*) or wood-putty patch (*page 122*).

Rubbing Out a Water Ring

Make an abrasive by mixing rottenstone powder with enough mineral oil to form a soft paste. Rub the paste into the damaged area with a folded pad of cheesecloth (*below*). If the ring does not disappear, use a stronger abrasive paste by substituting fine-grade pumice for the rottenstone. But be sure to rub gently — pumice applied with too much pressure may gouge wood.

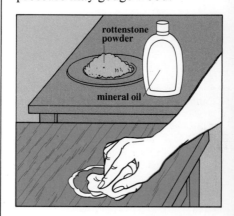

rottenstone powder

mineral oil

A Shellac-Stick Patch

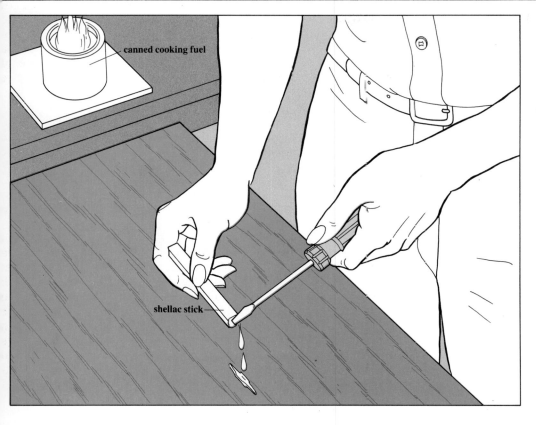

1 **Melting a shellac stick.** Set a small can of cooking fuel — the type used to heat chafing dishes — on a scrap of wood on a convenient work surface. Light the fuel with a match. Heat the blade of a screwdriver, paring knife or putty knife — whichever is closest in width to the size of the hole — in the flame for about 30 seconds. Holding the end of a shellac stick over the damaged area, apply the heated blade to the end to melt the shellac. Drip the molten shellac into the hole — reheating the blade as necessary — until the hole is slightly overfilled.

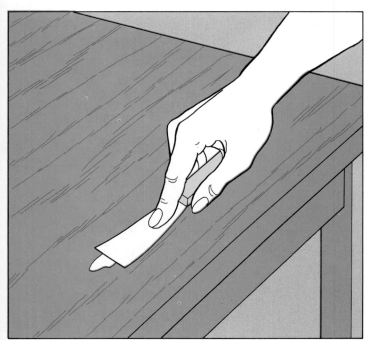

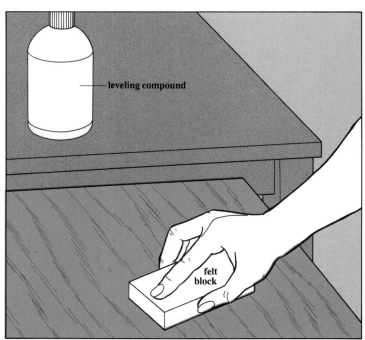

2 **Smoothing the shellac.** Before the molten shellac hardens, level its surface with a clean putty knife. Be careful not to spread the shellac beyond the damaged area. If the shellac hardens before you finish, liquefy it again by reheating the screwdriver or knife blade as described in Step 1. Let the shellac harden for a few minutes, then carefully scrape off excess little by little with a single-edged razor blade.

3 **Leveling the shellac.** Wet a thick block of rubbing felt with shellac-stick leveling compound or denatured alcohol. Rub the block across the hardened shellac to dissolve the top layer. Continue rubbing until the shellac is just flush with the surrounding surface. Be careful not to rub too long: The compound or alcohol might dissolve the wood's finish.

Concealing a Putty Patch

1 **Spreading the wood putty.** Using a putty knife, fill the damaged area with wood putty to a level slightly higher than the surface of the wood. Wait for the putty to dry enough so that a gentle push with your fingernail will not dent it. This may take from 30 minutes to several hours, depending on the depth of the patch. After the patch has dried, sand it lightly, first with medium (100-grit) sandpaper, then with fine (150-grit) sandpaper. Wipe up the putty dust with a cloth dampened in turpentine.

wood putty

2 **Staining the wood putty.** To provide a base for padding stain, wipe a coat of padding finish over the patch with a cheesecloth pad *(below)*. While the padding finish is still wet, dip the cheesecloth pad into the padding-stain powder, and dab the powder onto the padding finish *(below, right)*. Let the padding finish dry. Then apply a second coat of padding finish.

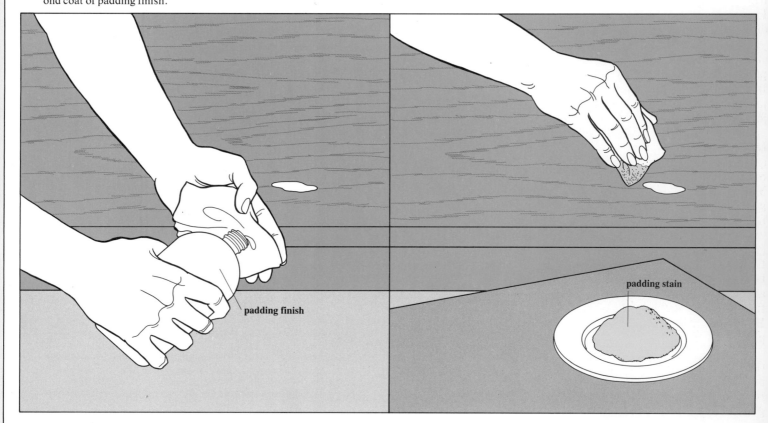

padding finish

padding stain

Repairing loose joints

Any piece of furniture requiring a new finish is likely to need some attention to its basic structure as well. As furniture ages, the glue that holds its joints together dries out. The result is a wobbly leg, a shaky arm, a rickety seat, a rattletrap drawer. Sometimes, a failing joint can be shored up with pieces of wood called glue blocks *(page 124)*. More often, the piece must be partially or totally taken apart, the old glue scraped off, new glue applied and the joint clamped tight until it is secure again.

The first step in this rehabilitation process is to determine the type of joint you are dealing with. The six most common ones are diagramed at right. They vary in complexity from the edge-glued butt joint *(top, near right)*, which relies solely on glue for its strength, to the dovetail joint *(top, far right)*, which is reinforced by intricate interlocking of its parts. In the other standard joints, extra bonding is provided by pegs and tongues that fit into matching holes and grooves.

Each of these joints can be knocked apart with a rubber mallet or "soft" hammer — a steel hammer whose head has been padded with several thicknesses of heavy cloth secured with rubber bands. First, however, check for fasteners, such as brads or nails, that must be removed. If you see cracking around the loose joint, stop. The cracks are warning signals that pulling the joint apart may split the wood. In such cases, or when only two or three joints are loose, you can often repair the joint with a glue injector *(page 124)*.

Before regluing a dismantled piece, remove the old glue thoroughly and reassemble the piece. This dry run will make the rest of the job go smoothly: You practice putting the pieces back together without fumbling and can check for further problems.

For indoor furniture, liquid hide glue *(page 102)* works best. It allows ample time — up to 20 minutes — for clamping before it begins to set and, when dry, it accepts paint and stain well. For outdoor furniture, use waterproof resorcinol glue. Both glues must be applied at room temperature and clamped for 12 hours.

Various clamps to apply pressure to the joint and keep it still can be bought at hardware stores or rented from tool-rental shops. Bar and pipe clamps are good for drawers, C clamps for arms or legs, and web clamps for an entire piece.

Common Furniture Joints

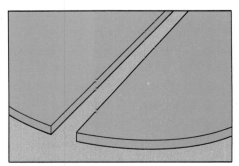

Edge-glued butt joint. Generally found where narrow pieces of wood are joined to form a wider piece — in tabletops or cabinet side panels, for example — this joint pulls apart when the wood shrinks with age. To repair it, remove the wide piece from its frame so that the joint can be completely separated and the old glue scraped off.

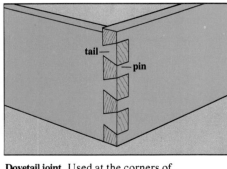

Dovetail joint. Used at the corners of drawers, this joint is formed by inserting a set of projecting wedges called tails into a set of correspondingly shaped cutouts called pins. Only the panel with the tails can move; to disassemble, reach inside the drawer and tap this side outward.

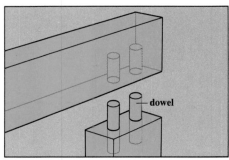

Dowel joint. This joint is commonly found where a chair arm meets an upright, and in other locations where the surfaces to be joined are small. Each dowel — a small cylinder of wood that fits into a matching hole — adds mechanical strength as well as providing more gluing surface.

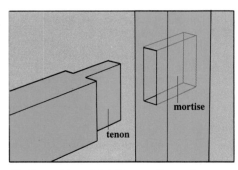

Mortise-and-tenon joint. Frequently used where furniture legs meet their frames, this joint is formed by inserting the tenon, or squared tongue, of one piece into the mortise, or squared cavity, of another piece.

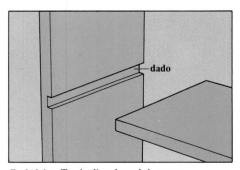

Dado joint. Typically, these joints are used to support shelves, drawer bottoms and partitions. The joint is formed by inserting the end of a solid board into the dado — a rectangular channel cut across the grain — of another piece. To separate the pieces, knock the solid board sideways.

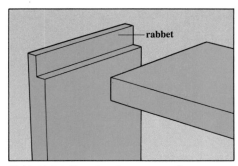

Rabbet joint. Found at the corners of many cabinets, where the top meets the sides, these joints are formed by fitting one piece of wood into a rectangular recess, or rabbet, cut out of the edge of another piece. Examine these joints carefully before dismantling them; they are sometimes nailed, screwed or pinned with dowels.

Regluing Loose Chair Rungs

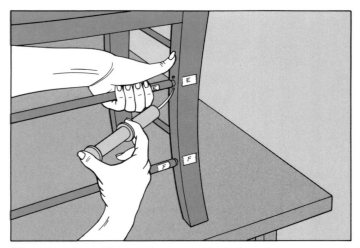

Using a glue injector. If two or three rungs of a chair are loose, you can reglue them without taking the chair apart. Pull out a loose rung partway and scrape off all the old glue you can reach with a penknife. Then, from above and below the socket for the rung, drill two 1/16-inch holes at angles into the socket. Insert the tip of a syringe-type glue injector, filled with liquid hide glue, into one hole at a time *(above)* and squeeze the plunger. Wiggle the rung to distribute the glue; then press the rung home. Some glue should ooze out of the joint. Wipe off the excess with a damp rag, and clamp the joint with a web clamp *(opposite, Step 3)*.

Glue Blocks for a Wobbly Table Leg

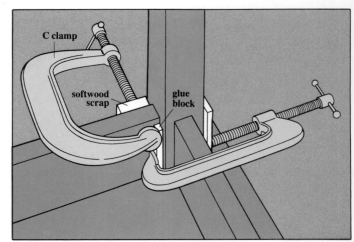

Clamping glue blocks. Turn the table upside down. Cut two rectangular blocks of wood to fit into the corners formed by the wobbly leg and the skirts. Sand off any dirt, glue or finish. Spread liquid hide glue on two adjacent sides of one glue block and press the block into the corner. Using softwood scraps to protect the surface, apply C clamps as shown above. After 12 hours, remove the clamps, and glue and clamp the second block in the other corner.

Regluing a Drawer Panel

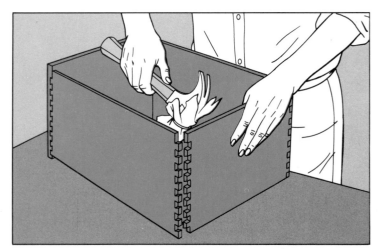

Knocking apart the drawer. Tap the dovetail joints apart with a rubber mallet or, as shown here, a soft hammer. Take care to drive the panel with the tails in the one direction in which it will move *(page 123)*. With a penknife, scrape off all the old glue. Refit the joint without glue. Then disassemble it again and with a small brush *(opposite, Step 4)* apply liquid hide glue to both surfaces of each dovetail joint. Reassemble the joint.

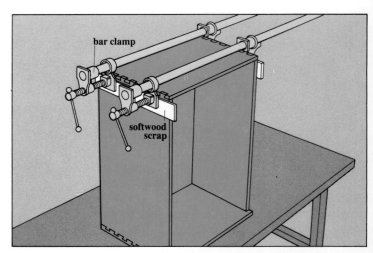

Clamping the drawer. To square the drawer, measure the diagonal distances across the open top of the drawer. If the diagonals differ, re-align the drawer as necessary to make the two distances equal. Once the drawer is square, apply bar clamps, as shown above.

Regluing All the Joints of a Chair

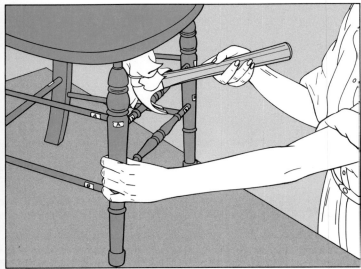

1 **Taking the chair apart.** Label each part of the chair with a lettered piece of masking tape, so that you will know how the parts go back together. Then tap the joints apart, using a soft hammer or rubber mallet. If a joint wiggles but does not come apart, look for nailheads on the sides of the legs at socket locations. With a sharp penknife, pare away wood from around the nailhead until you can pull the nail with pliers or a claw hammer. To separate a stubborn joint that is not pinned, cushion one part with scraps of softwood and clamp the wood in a vise; then, using firmer blows, knock the joint apart.

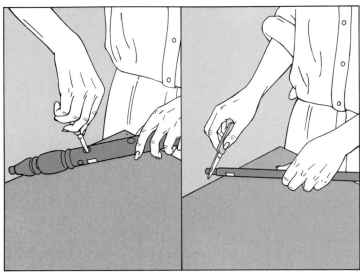

2 **Removing old glue.** With the blade of a penknife, scrape the old glue out of the mortises and sockets (*above, left*) and off the tenons and rungs (*above, right*). Coarse sandpaper can also be used to remove old glue, but be careful not to sand the underlying wood: Otherwise, the rungs may no longer fit snugly in the sockets.

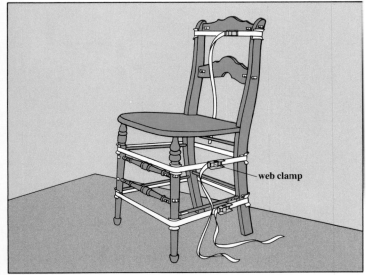

web clamp

3 **Making a dry run.** Working without glue, reassemble the chair. Check each joint for snugness; try to slide the tenons side to side and rotate the rungs. Mark the extra-loose joints with masking tape and for each one, cut two strips of cheesecloth, 3 inches long and ½ inch wide. Then truss the chair securely with web clamps, placing protective cushions of cardboard or scraps of carpet between the web and the chair as shown above. Now undo all the clamps and take the chair apart again. You are ready to glue.

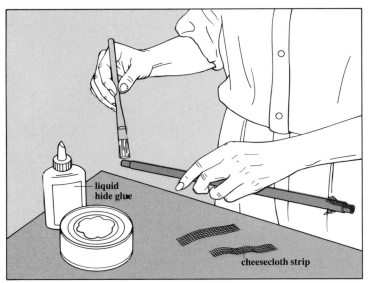

liquid hide glue

cheesecloth strip

4 **Regluing the joints.** Pour an ounce of liquid hide glue into a shallow container, such as the bottom of an inverted tin can. Start with the extra-loose joints: With a small brush, coat the surfaces of the joint with glue. Then lay one cheesecloth strip over the end of the rung and refit the joint. If it is still loose, undo it and add a second strip, at right angles to the first. Reassemble the joint and cut off excess cloth. Apply glue to all the other joints, assemble the chair and clamp it, making sure that all joints are seated well and the chair sits level. Wipe off excess glue. Fill nail holes and scars with wood putty.

Acknowledgments

The index for this book was prepared by Louise Hedberg. The editors wish to thank the following persons and institutions: Marirosa Ballo, Studio Ballo, Milan; Carla De Benedetti, Milan; Henri Boiton, Thonet Frère, Le Mée-sur-Seine, France; Royal A. Brown, Vienna, Virginia; Sandy Cohen, Albany State College, Albany, Georgia; Jean Delmas, École Boulle, Paris; Larry C. Denney, The Cop Shop, Arlington, Virginia; Robert Falotico Studios, New York; Jacques Gausserand, École Boulle, Paris; Walter Grazzani, Studio Azzurro, Milan; Mary Madeline King, The Stenciled Pineapple, Falls Church, Virginia; Carol Martell, Gaithersburg, Maryland; Catherine O'Grady, The Stenciled Pineapple, Falls Church, Virginia; Andrée Putman, Paris; Frederick W. Sachs Jr., W. A. Smoot & Co. Inc., Alexandria, Virginia; Stephen Vance, Distinctive Bookbinding, Washington, D.C.

Picture Credits

The sources for the photographs in this book are listed below, followed by the sources for the illustrations. Credits from left to right on a single page or a two-page spread are separated by semicolons; credits from top to bottom are separated by dashes.

Photographers: **Cover:** Fil Hunter, photographer / rug from Bill's Carpet Warehouse, Alexandria, Virginia. **2, 3:** Jacques Dirand, photographer, reprinted from *French Style* by Suzanne Slesin, Stafford Cliff and Jacques Dirand, copyright 1982 by Suzanne Slesin, Stafford Cliff and Jacques Dirand. Used by permission of Clarkson N. Potter. **4, 5:** Michael Boys Syndication, Woodbridge, Suffolk, photographer; Michael Boys from Susan Griggs Agency, London, photographer. **6:** Emmett Bright, photographer, courtesy Piero Sartogo, Rome. **7:** Michael Dunne from Elizabeth Whiting & Associates, London, photographer / Alan Buchsbaum, architect. **8, 9:** Giovanna Piemonti, Rome, photographer; Guy Bouchet, Paris, photographer. **10, 11:** John Corcoran, photographer, courtesy *Early American Life*. **28-42:** Fil Hunter, photographer. **44:** Larry Sherer, photographer. **46-52:** Fil Hunter, photographer. **54:** Philadelphia Museum of Art: The Titus C. Geesey Collection. **55:** © The Henry Francis du Pont Winterthur Museum — Philadelphia Museum of Art: The Titus C. Geesey Collection — © The Henry Francis du Pont Winterthur Museum. **56-84:** Fil Hunter, photographer. **89:** Fil Hunter, photographer / veneer by Albert Constantine and Son, Inc., Bronx, New York. **90:** Larry Sherer, photographer. **95:** Larry Sherer, photographer / veneer by Albert Constantine and Son, Inc., Bronx, New York; inset, Fil Hunter, photographer. **96:** Larry Sherer, photographer. **100:** Fil Hunter, photographer / inlay by Craftsman Wood Service Co., Addison, Illinois. **103:** Larry Sherer, photographer / inlay by Craftsman Wood Service Co., Addison, Illinois. **106:** Fil Hunter, photographer / gold by Basic Crafts Co. Bookbinding, New York. **114:** Fil Hunter, photographer; Larry Sherer, photographer.
Illustrations: **17-19:** Sketches by George Bell, inked by John Massey. **21:** Sketches by William J. Hennessy Jr., inked by Arezou Katoozian. **22-25:** Sketches by Kathy Rebeiz, inked by Frederic F. Bigio from B-C Graphics. **27, 31:** Sketches by Joan McGurren, inked by Marc Levenson. **33:** Sketches by Jack Arthur, inked by Elsie J. Hennig. **34, 35:** Sketches by Kathy Rebeiz, inked by Frederic F. Bigio from B-C Graphics. **41:** Sketches and inking by William J. Hennessy Jr. **43-49:** Sketches by Joan McGurren, inked by Marc Levenson. **50-53:** Sketches by William J. Hennessy Jr., inked by Frederic F. Bigio from B-C Graphics. **57-60:** Sketches by Fred Holz, inked by Frederic F. Bigio from B-C Graphics. **62, 63:** Sketches by Joan McGurren, inked by Stephen Turner. **65-69:** Sketches by William J. Hennessy Jr., inked by Adisai Hemintranont from Sai Graphis. **71-73:** Sketches by Kathy Rebeiz, inked by Marc Levenson. **75-83:** William J. Hennessy Jr., inked by Eduino Pereira. **85-87:** Sketches by Fred Holz, inked by Elsie J. Hennig. **91-94:** Sketches by Kathy Rebeiz, inked by Elsie J. Hennig. **97-99:** Sketches by Fred Holz, inked by Adisai Hemintranont from Sai Graphis. **101:** Sketches by Jack Arthur, inked by Adisai Hemintranont from Sai Graphis. **102-105:** Sketches by Jack Arthur, inked by Elsie J. Hennig. **107-113:** Sketches by Joan McGurren, inked by Adisai Hemintranont from Sai Graphis. **115-119:** Sketches by Fred Holz, inked by Frederic F. Bigio from B-C Graphics. **120-122:** Sketches by Jack Arthur, inked by Adisai Hemintranont from Sai Graphis. **123:** Sketches by Fred Holz, inked by Adisai Hemintranont from Sai Graphis. **124, 125:** Sketches by Fred Holz, inked by Arezou Katoozian.

Index/Glossary

Time-Life Books Inc. offers a wide range of fine recordings, including a *Big Bands* series. For subscription information, call 1-800-621-7026, or write TIME-LIFE MUSIC, Time & Life Building, Chicago, Illinois 60611.